ept

Jean-Paul Sartre: His Philosophy

Jean-Paul Sartre:
His Philosophy

René Lafarge

Translated by Marina Smyth-Kok

UNIVERSITY OF NOTRE DAME PRESS

Contents

Preface

Though it is a great honor to present this study, it would have been much better if another had done it in my stead. This is easily understood, especially when I tell you that the "other" I have in mind is a first-rate philosopher: Jacques Maritain, who once had René Lafarge as a student. He read the first drafts of this work and gave invaluable advice in its composition. We are therefore not surprised to find the author quoting extensively from Maritain's works in the last pages of this book, when he wishes to express the essential points of his personal position towards Sartre's doctrine. It would have been most desirable that the master write the preface to a work in which he is given such an important role.

Unfortunately for us, Maritain has sought, in the Toulouse house of the sons of the Père de Foulcauld, a jealously protected retreat. Though he now lives away from the world, he still receives numerous echoes of what is going on outside, especially in intellectual and religious circles; he knows them better than anyone and, on occasion, speaks up about them in a most authoritative fashion. (We need only recall *Le Paysan de la Garonne* and the turmoil its actuality created.) But the author of the present study felt it would not be fitting to burden his one-time teacher with the writing of this preface.

If he chose me instead, it is—as one might suspect—because of this *Existentialisme* which is still enjoying in the Collection *Que Sais-je?* a popularity which does not cease to amaze me. The reason for this success must lie in the following comment by Cardinal Saliège. To someone who remarked, "This, your Eminence, is an extremely clear little book," he replied, "Yes indeed, it is clear; it is even too clear." It is true that it was not written for specialists in philosophy who are quite justified in feeling it is over-simplified; it was intended for the wider audience which, after the Liberation, was begging for conferences to enlighten it on this new philosophy.

René Lafarge tells us that the *Sartre* we are now introducing has the same origin. It grew out of lectures he gave at the time when the author of *Being and Nothingness* was enjoying "an exceptionally wide audience." However, owing to various circumstances, he did not think of publishing his work then. It is quite some time later that people who had heard his talks and friends succeeded in convincing him of their interest. And thus this book appears, in a sense, with a delay of several years.

But only in a sense. In fact, a critic of the original conferences might well have said, "It is all too clear." However, the present *Sartre* does not suffer from this weakness. The author had time to increase his knowledge of the problems and of their answers, to become acquainted with the extensive literature that arose out of existentialism, and to reread the essential texts. Moreover, he has been able to make use of the works which Sartre published after *Being and Nothingness,* more especially his *Critique of Dialectical Reason* (1960). Certain chroniclers, in presenting that work, have been content to read only the important introductory article, *The Problem of Method.* René Lafarge read the entire work, and his last chapter (regarding Sartre's ontology), gives an account of his findings and completes his exposition.

Lafarge avoids the obscurity which some people feel has become the main feature of any serious philosophical work. His experience in teaching philosophy has accustomed him to exigencies which are less imperative for those whose main goal is to inform reasonably well-educated readers of the doctrines currently in vogue. He desires above all to be understood. He therefore abolishes hermetic terms and speaks in everyday language as much as possible. He also distinguishes the various philosophical points with great care, considering them in an order which he tries to make apparent. This *Sartre* is therefore especially well suited to students in philosophy who wish to gain a comprehensive view of the doctrine of the author of *Being and Nothingness*.

It is this latter work, naturally, which is referred to most often. But Lafarge also makes use of the plays and novels which many times provide a more tangible illustration of an abstract thought. He frequently uses *Nausea,* an excellent choice, since the experience of Roquentin provides a relatively easy introduction not only to the views of phenomenologists but also to those of metaphysicians with respect to the ontological problems of being. He rather aptly calls his first chapter "*Nausea* and the Revelation of Being," returning toward the end of his study to this most unusual novel in order to extract from it those famous phrases which express with such intensity the essential theses of Sartre's phenomenological ontology and of the ethic that follows from it.

In view of his audience, the author could not be satisfied with an objective exposition which would more or less let his readers believe that *Being and Nothingness* provides a satisfactory solution to problems philosophers cannot agree on. But apart from the last few pages which display the paralogisms in Sartrian atheism, this study is essentially positive. If he reduces the paradoxes which Sartre opposes to traditional concepts to their true value, he does not underestimate this value nor the revival which these paradoxes brought about in philosophical thought.

René Lafarge's study is neither an unconditional adhesion nor a peremptory rejection, but measured reflections allowing for personal judgment: a very timely appraisal.

P. Foulquie

Introduction

From its very first appearance in contemporary thought, Sartrian existentialism met with tremendous success. At a time when the world was going through an agonizing crisis—the sombre days of the Second World War were just over—and when most traditional values were treated with scorn, it was not surprising that the philosopher of lucidity and of the absurd should, quite naturally, find a receptive audience, and this is precisely what happened. In fact, Sartre's following sometimes would be such as not to please him very much.

We must try to visualize 1946 when, we are laughingly told, "there was no hostess, whether in France, Argentina, Italy or Peru, who would fail to draw her 'intellectual' guest to a quiet corner and say, 'My dear Sir, let us now talk about your Sartre, and tell me, in five minutes, what existentialism is all about.'"[1] It is certain that Sartre had become "the teacher of the entire world," as Jean Guitton put it in his *Dialogues avec Monsieur Pouget,* and that his name was to be found everywhere, on stage, on the screen and in bookstore windows. Snobbishness? Most certainly, and not always in the best taste either, but in spite of its excesses, or precisely because of them, it was the sign that philosophy was speaking of something serious.

On the subject of existentialism Gilson wrote:

It is often said that contemporary existentialism owes its success to the whim of a passing fashion. I do not think so. For the first time in quite a while, philosophy has decided to speak of serious matters and, to tell the truth,

there would be good reason to despair if the general public had not noticed it. Whatever their mode of expression, these thinkers who are conveniently referred to as
existentialists are most definitely not amateurs playing
with ideas. Passionately concerned with the most intimate aspects of the real, they cling to it obstinately, even
if it hurts them; and if blood flows with such sincerity
in their works, it is because their own is very often
mingled with it. Existence is sacred to them, all contact
with it is unbearable, and all the resources of what Pascal
terms 'distractions' scarcely suffice to protect us from it;
if there is anything in this world that is divine, we must
search for it here, and no one can come close to it without feeling a genuine religious terror, in an experience
which involves his whole being, in which the body itself
is vitally concerned.[2]

Cannot Gilson's views on existentialism be applied
more specifically to Sartre? There seems little doubt but
they can. Philosophers until then, whether of an idealistic
or a materialistic bent, had only too often created the impression that they had nothing to do with concrete reality,
with "the creature of flesh and soul who lives, struggles
and suffers." They set up systems and rebuilt the world in
terms of abstract principles, without any real concern "for
direct and personal contact with reality." The spider was
intent only on weaving its web. It was not surprising therefore that all these clever games of the mind should have
seemed remote from the profound exigencies of the
human person.[3]

Now Sartre belongs to a tradition which shuns the
abstract as much as it possibly can, and tries to remain
glued to the real.[4] He did not wish to build a system, but
rather to unveil the most intimate and most mysterious

aspects of existence. For when he spoke of existence, it was of human existence he spoke, the only one that exists in his view. He appeared as a man speaking to men, whom he had a passion to understand. Did he not write in *Saint Genêt:* "Whatever mistakes I may make about him, I am sure that I know him better than he knows himself because I have a passion for understanding men."[5] And in a letter to Garaudy, after reproaching him with his narrow and sclerotic Marxism: "We are concerned with men, and I fear that you have somewhat forgotten about them."[6]

Now, if this is the case, we must not be surprised that Sartre's views had their moment of glory, and that they continue, now that the turmoil has abated, to arouse comments and questions; and not only among young radicals as one would have us believe! However, as it appears in its amazing diversity, in his philosophical works, his plays, his fiction, his essays, and even in his political stands, can it truly be called a philosophy? We would not have raised this question had Sartre himself not done it and if his answer did not allow us to clarify his position with respect to Marxism and contemporary Marxists.

Existentialism and Marxism

What is philosophy? According to Sartre, it is self-consciousness (i.e. consciousness [of] self), the mirror of "the rising class." It appears as "the totalization of contemporary knowledge. The philosopher effects the unification of everything that is known, following certain guiding schemata which express the attitudes and techniques of the rising class regarding its own period and world."[7]

It is obvious, then, that philosophies come and go, but at any one time there can only be one that is truly efficacious, that which is engendered and supported by *praxis* and which clarifies it. That one which is gradually transformed and loses its uniqueness and finally "impregnates the masses . . . so as to become in and through them a collective instrument of emancipation."

Under these conditions, periods of philosophical creations are rare indeed. Sartre sees only three of them from the seventeenth to the twentieth century, and designates them by means of the most famous names within these periods.

> There is the 'moment' of Descartes and Locke, that of Kant and Hegel, finally that of Marx. These three philosophies become, each in its turn, the humus of every particular thought and the horizon of all culture; there is no going beyond them so long as man has not gone beyond the historical moment which they express. I have often remarked on the fact that an 'anti-Marxist' argument is only the apparent rejuvenation of a pre-Marxist Idea. A so-called 'going beyond' Marxism will be at worst only a return to pre-Marxism; at best, only the rediscovery of a thought already contained in the philosophy which one believes he has gone beyond.[8]

There are men, however, who come after the great flowering and who undertake to set the systems in order, to carry out further investigations and determine possible practical applications. They explore the domain and "may even bring about certain internal changes; but they still get their nourishment from the living thought of the great dead." Can these be called philosophers? Sartre thinks not. He prefers to call them "ideologists." And thus existentialism, which has always been and still is a "parasitical system living in the margin of Knowledge," is not strictly speaking a philosophy. What then is its function, its justification, as an ideology?

In the days of Hegelianism, the question did not arise. Knowledge, raised to its most eminent dignity, did not view Being from the outside. It incorporated it, and dissolved it in itself. And when dealing with man, it pierced him through and through, so to speak, integrating him in the supreme totalization. Thus for Hegel "the pure, lived aspect of a tragic experience, a suffering unto death, is absorbed by the system as a relatively abstract determination which must be mediated, as a passage toward the Absolute, the only genuine concrete."[9]

It is therefore not surprising that a Christian such as Kierkegaard should have taken a strong stand against Hegel, unrelentingly and passionately asserting "the irreducibility and the specificity of what is lived." It was necessary that existentialism set itself up against the system; on this score, Kierkegaard was absolutely right.

> Grief, need, passion, the pain of men are brute realities which can neither be surpassed nor changed by knowledge. To be sure, Kierkegaard's religious subjectivism can with good reason be taken as the very peak of idealism; but in relation to Hegel, he marks a progress toward realism, since he insists above all on the *primacy* of the specifically real over thought, that the real cannot be reduced to thought.[10]

In relation to Hegel it is beyond doubt: a reality had to be preserved, and not a negligible one either. But though this existential reaction had its purpose yesterday, is it still valid now, in the period of Marx? It would seem not, since the synthesis of the conflicting doctrines has been realized. Just like Kierkegaard, Marx proclaims the "specificity of human existence"; like Hegel he reaches "the concrete man in his objective reality," so that not only does he go beyond Hegelianism but he also goes beyond existentialism.

And yet, Kierkegaard's ideology survives. Must we see this as the mere survival of an idealism that refuses to die and the final effort—doomed to failure—to resuscitate the transcendent? Sartre thinks so in the case of a doctrine such as that of Jaspers, whose subjective pessimism "ultimately emerges as a theological optimism that dare not speak its name."[11]

But there is a form of existentialism to which this reproach does not apply. And that is atheistic existentialism; that form of existentialism remains necessary, at least for the time being, so long as Marxism is still ailing.

For Marxism is currently suffering from sclerosis. Marx had put concrete man at the center of his research, "that man who is defined simultaneously by his needs, by the material conditions of his existence, and by the nature of his work—that is, by his struggle against things and against men."[12] But the movement of Marxism has stopped. Not through an aging process, for it is still very young and only beginning its course, but because of the circumstances that accompanied its development. There arose men who wanted to change the world and whose philosophy, because it was *practical*, gave rise to a "veritable schism which rejected theory on one side and *praxis* on the other." The exigencies of action prompted them to integrate the group to the limit, and consequently to refuse all discussions which would have promoted the cause of truth. They put the doctrine out of the reach of experience, whereas "concrete thought must be born from *praxis* and must turn back upon it in order to clarify it."

This unwarranted separation resulted in transforming practice into an empiricism without principles, and theory into a pure, fixed knowledge.[13]

We are therefore forced to acknowledge that

> today social and historical experience falls outside of Knowledge. Bourgeois concepts just manage to revive and quickly break down; those which survive lack any foundation. The real attainments of American sociology cannot hide its theoretic uncertainty. Psychoanalysis, after a spectacular beginning, has stood still. It knows a great many details, but it lacks any firm foundation. Marxism possesses theoretical bases, it embraces all human activity; but it no longer *knows* anything. Its concepts are *dictates*; its goal is no longer to increase what it knows but to be itself constituted a priori as an absolute Knowledge. In view of this twofold ignorance, existentialism has been able to return and to maintain itself because it reaffirmed the reality of men as Kierkegaard asserted his own reality against Hegel.[14]

We are thus warned that whether it be a philosophy or an ideology (the distinction, though of importance to Sartre, is in fact of little consequence), existentialism is necessary in contemporary thought and will remain so as long as Marxism does not speak enough of man or does not speak well about him. For it is up to existentialism to fill the gap; and this it does. But how? In other words, what is this human reality which present-day Marxists persist in overlooking?

Sartre's Man

Sartre, anxious to give us the answer to this question, already does it throughout his extensive literary work. But to get an accurate idea of man as he sees him, it is to his philosophical works we must turn, more especially to *Being and Nothingness.* An ambitious work, *Being and Nothingness* attempts to account for the whole of reality. It is an ontology—a phenomenological ontology, written in 1943, when Sartre was influenced by Husserl.

Sartre attempts to describe "the world and consciousness as they appear, with the basic idea that it is in this apparition (and not appearance, which would imply the existence of something *underneath*) that reality must lie. A thing is that which appears to me, and nothing else. The world is the totality of what appears to consciousness, consciousness is both the apprehension of this apparition and that which appears to itself in the act of apprehension . . . it is therefore in emerging to the world that consciousness finds itself." Sartre writes, "It is not in some hidden retreat that we will find ourselves, but on the road." We will no longer tolerate an external world on the one side, an "inner life" on the other. There will no longer be the appearance of things on the surface and "reality-in-itself" somewhere else.[15]

We must make one distinction however, that of the *In-itself* and the *For-itself.* On the one side, is Being properly so-called, opaque and solid, being identical with itself, the thing, of which one can only affirm the reality. On the other, is consciousness which never coincides with itself. A perpetual wrenching away from Being, on which and beyond which it constantly projects itself, it is a freedom that makes itself and, in so doing, discovers itself and discovers the world, for there can be an In-itself only in terms of a For-itself.

The object of *Being and Nothingness* is thus essentially the description of freedom in all its modalities. It is the study of man—man at grips with the In-itself and carnal contingency; man at grips with the Other and his unbearable presence.

However, when dealing with human reality, knowledge is not enough. It is true that ontology is necessary, but it is not an end in itself. It is a step in an evolution.[16] For man as he appears is an ambiguous reality: he is free and yet must free himself, he is man and yet must humanize himself, so that ontology calls for an ethic. This is what Sartre thinks, he who wrote "Since the existent is for me a being who 'must exist its being,' it is clear that ontology cannot be separated from ethics."[17] And yet, after so many years we are still waiting for this ethic.

It is true that we know what it should be. We know this from certain revealing passages in *Being and Nothingness,* and mostly from the extensions they were given by Simone de Beauvoir in *Pyrrhus et Cinéas* and in *Pour une morale de l'ambiguité.* It cannot be a "piece of nonsense" fit only to lull our consciousness, but must consist of wanting to be free, of wanting the others to be free, and of always acting so as to ensure this.

But however precious these clues, they do not constitute Sartre's ethic. Will we ever be given this ethic which would fix the principles behind our actions? To venture a precise answer, we must turn to his *Critique of Dialectical Reason* which combines with *Being and Nothingness* to throw some light on the matter.

In 1960, Sartre lays the foundations of a vast anthropology which is to be continued, but which, from the very beginning, sets man in his historical condition—and freedom before history. The perspective of ontology then broadens. The world appears simultaneously as:

"My project itself, in the process of being carried out on the objects I am transforming.

". . . a universe of mostly inert matter, already worked upon by men.

". . . and because of this work, a tight web of already constituted relations in which I am situated."[18]

Therefore, no sooner does my freedom arise than it is struck with *alienation;* set in a climate of scarcity and violence, its project escapes it and can no longer recognize itself in the results of action. We remain free, but our freedom is constantly betrayed. It is real and yet ever impotent.

How then can we speak of ethics, since we do not control our actions, since our freedom "vanishes into thin air" as we are exercising it. And yet, morality is unavoidable. Unavoidable and impossible.

Unavoidable—in that alienated freedom is still freedom and every man, in a Godless world, is at all times responsible for the whole world. But impossible because we cannot imagine today what the world of a free man would be like; even our values are tied up with the world they are contesting.

The only valid imperative today must be to take disalienated freedom as our end, to strive toward disalienation, that is, to fight against the existing social order.[19]

And this, we must admit, is already an ethic, a temporary ethic—valid while we are awaiting the final ethic that will be established when the historical condition changes, if it ever does, and which we cannot predict it will be. This is how Sartre's man appears to us after the investigations of the *Critique of Dialectal Reason.*

He is in the paradoxical situation of having "to be

what he is" and yet it is impossible for him to do this—at least for the time being, as long as ethic will be faulty (as it will be until the reign of freedom has come). But that which is presented to us as temporary and perhaps still allows for hope to creep in—might it not turn out to be definitive? In other words, will this man of Sartre's, unable to humanize himself in his present condition, be able to do it tomorrow? Is there perhaps even some imperative that is valid today, if only that of making freedom our end and fighting against the established social order? This question must be answered in the negative; and this is why.

A Statement of Failure

Unless we consent to a voluntarism without justification—which would be quite a feat—there can be no moral imperative except referred to some absolute. Whatever our situation and the tasks that befall us, if everything is contingent there is no reason for giving life a meaning.

Francis Jeanson, one of the foremost authorities on Sartre's thought (so that his opinion is of great importance) does not hesitate to acknowledge this. He wrote:

> However much I may be situated, however much I may be committed, I still have to commit myself. Were I to belong to the ranks of the starving, I still would have to choose whether to fight for survival or resign myself to die; and we who are hardly threatened by death, in the name of what could we become true revolutionaries? Why trouble to change the world if everything is relative, if the only absolute in our condition is this ineluctable end which is imposed upon us from without.[20]

In the same way, supposing the historical situation

should change and freedom does reach someday the plenitude of its power, why should it take itself as an end? Is
this absolute, which is necessary to morality, to be found
in the thought of Sartre?

Francis Jeanson tries to convince us that it is. For him
the absolute is no other than a wager, the

> gamble on man and by each man, above all on himself.
> Either this life is nothing or else it must be everything;
> by considering the possibility of losing it rather than
> submitting it to the absurd, we set up *an absolute point
> of reference* at the very heart of our existence, a fixed
> point where we can cast our anchor and the possibility
> of a meaning for all our concrete enterprises. . . . The
> absolute, in this sense . . . is but our choice to exist, to
> be ever more present to ourselves and to others.[21]

Would Sartre adopt this argumentation? What is certain is that it is not very convincing. We do not understand that one can talk of an absolute in connection with
an arbitrary choice, an uncertain wager. Of course, one
can want life to be everything, and prefer to lose it rather
than subject it to the absurd. One can also gamble on
man—but it remains that the choice is precarious and the
wager risky. This is no absolute point of reference, nor
this "human exigency of humanization" which Jeanson
sometimes says is necessary to ethics.

In reality, Sartre's ontology excludes the absolute. And,
it would appear, quite irrevocably. The following pages
will prove this. They will first place us before the observation that *Being* is the *In-itself*, contingent and "de trop,"
and that consciousness exists—and also the world—only
to the extent that it denies it, living thus in a continual

state of tension; for at the same time that it rejects being, it is also fascinated by it.

Consequently, man will appear as a

> being condemned to the world, made from a relation to this world, without whom there would be no world and yet ever elsewhere, endlessly denying himself in a perpetual flight forward: an ambiguous reality, which is simultaneously "de trop," which exists as a body in an obscene superabundance, and which, as consciousness and 'for-itself' is inconsistent, empty, complete lack of being . . . a subject in a situation, at the mercy of the countless fatalities of nature and history, expropriated, inhabited, haunted by the others without ever being able to communicate with anyone, free but for nothing, of an absolute freedom that makes him completely responsible for himself and for the world.[22]

And yet we see this torn and impotent being searching endlessly for the justification of his existence. We see him ever ready to put his freedom in the hands of some natural, social, or divine necessity. And thus it will sink into bad faith, which is the ontological malady of consciousness. He will go from failure to failure: failure before the In-itself, before the others, and before himself, without being able to do anything about it. For freedom, the creator of all values, will never find a "fixed point where it can cast its anchor," nor the possibility of a meaning for its enterprises. Man therefore will go on floundering in contradiction: condemned to make himself, he will not be able to do it.

Sartre's ontology is a statement of failure, but such a statement must be carefully examined. Is human reality really what they say? And in order to preserve freedom, must we refuse to inscribe it in an order beyond it, as contemporary humanists are inclined to do? We can already say that our answer will be negative.

Sartre is a splendid example of an exceptional talent and a generous will put to the service of man. But he felt he should reject Being, and with it Good and Truth, and this led him to a dead end from which he is trying in vain to escape. What he considered our salvation is in fact our damnation.

Is this refusal to which Sartre's ontology leads us legitimate? We do not think so and we will give our reasons in the conclusion to this study.

NOTES

1. R.M. Albérès, *Les Nouvelles Littéraires*, July 9, 1964, p. 5.
2. Gustave Thibon, *Revue de Philosophie*, 2nd ed. (1946), pp. 144–145.
3. Etienne Gilson, *L'Etre et l'Essence*, Problemes et controverses (Paris, 1948), pp. 297–298.
4. Cf. Paul Foulquié, *L'Existentialisme* (Collection *Que Sais-je?*); Emmanuel Mounier, *Introduction aux Existentialismes*; Jean Wahl, *Esquisse pour une Histoire de l'Existentialisme*; Roger Verneaux, *Lecons sur l'Existentialisme* (1st and 2nd eds.).
5. Jean-Paul Sartre, *Saint Genet: Actor and Martyr* (New York: George Braziller, 1963), p. 137.
6. R. Garaudy, *Perspectives de l'Homme*, Bibliotheque de philosophie contemporaine (Paris, 1960), p. 113.
7. Jean-Paul Sartre, *The Problem of Method*, translation of the prefatory essay in *Critique de la Raison Dialectique* (New York: Knopf, 1963), p. 4.
8. *Ibid.*, p. 7.
9. *Ibid.*, p. 9.
10. *Ibid.*, p. 12.
11. *Ibid.*, p. 16.
12. *Ibid.*, p. 14.
13. *Ibid.*, p. 22.
14. *Ibid.*, p. 28.
15. Colette Audry, *Connaissance de Sartre* (Paris, 1955), pp. 11–12.
16. Cf. Jacques Maritain, *Moral Philosophy* (New York: Scribner's, 1964), pp. 370 *et seq.*
17. Francis Jeanson, *Le Problème Moral et la Pensée de Sartre*, Lettre preface, Collection Pensée et civilisation (Paris, 1947), p. 14.
18. Colette Audry, *op. cit.*, p. 83.

19. *Ibid.*, pp. 112–113.
20. Francis Jeanson, *op. cit.*, nouvelle edition, pp. 344–345.
21. *Ibid.*, p. 345.
22. Etienne Borne, *Témoignage Chrétien*, no. 1145, June 1966, p. 15.

(I)

Nausea *and the Revelation*
of Being

We do not often have the opportunity of approaching philosophy with the help of a novel. But Sartre's *Nausea* does just this. Through the pathetic pages of his journal, we follow the tribulations of an imaginary hero, and the gradual unfolding of a strange experience brings us in the presence of Being and its mystery.

After extensive travels, Antoine Roquentin has come to settle in Bouville, with the intention of working there. Interested in a fascinating and shifty character of the eighteenth century, the Marquis de Rollebon, Roquentin has heard that he would find all documents necessary to his investigations in the library of that town. It matters little whether it is the love of work or the call of a new adventure that draws him there. What we do know is that the weary traveler has become a hardworking and solitary scholar.

He is solitary above all, for during the three years he spends in Bouville, he makes no friends and does not seek

after any. It is true that he visits with the obliging patron-
ess of the "Railwaymen's Rendezvous," but he sees no
point in talking to her. The words they exchange are so
trite that there is no hope for true dialogue. The same is
true of the old phoney of a Self-Taught Man whom he
often meets. This man, once a bailiff's clerk, has the peculiar habit of going through all the books in the library
one after the other, scrupulously observing the alphabeti-
cal order of their authors' names. What can one do with
such a strange character but have fun at the admiration he
feels for you, and (to thank him for it) to listen benevo-
lently, though absentmindedly, to his chatter, just carefully enough to satisfy the requirements of a tolerant
politeness.

As for the patrons of the restaurants and cafés he fre-
quents, Roquentin examines them with curiosity, making
passing notes of the picturesque or the ridiculous in their
gestures or conversations. But nothing in them attracts
him in any way. They leave him indifferent, as does the
whole town: a tasteless mixture of old and new which he
scarcely notices. Antoine Roquentin has shut himself up
in solitude and silence, and thus is in the best possible
condition to complete his scholarly task. Or so it seems.

A Strange Experience

And yet this calm is but an appearance, a front. It is in
his attitudes, but not in his soul. For he suffers from a
peculiar ailment which has begun quite suddenly, rather
unobtrusively, like one of those diseases which do not at
first betray their seriousness. There were some children on
the beach, playing ducks and drakes. He felt like doing
the same and picked up a pebble, but stopped short. The

pebble slipped out of his hand as he tried to hold it back. He had suddenly been overcome by an unpleasant sensation, a sort of sweetish sickness.

Naturally he did not attach much importance to this incident and would have completely forgotten about it had the phenomenon not occurred over and over again, leaving him most perplexed. In spite of his efforts to convince himself that this was not possible, it soon became obvious that the world was changing around him.

Of course he was still in the same room, looking out on the Rue des Mutilés below and on the construction yard of the new station. And a little further off, at the corner of the Boulevard Victor-Noir, there was still the red and white flame of the "Railwaymen's Rendezvous" and the Paris train coming in, pouring its numerous passengers pell-mell onto the platform. The objects around him and everywhere were the same as before, but these very objects were gradually taking on a singular and disconcerting appearance.

A little while ago, just as I was coming into my room, I stopped short because I felt in my hand a cold object which held my attention through a sort of personality. I opened my hand, looked: I was simply holding the doorknob. This morning in the library, when the Self-Taught Man came to say good morning to me, it took me ten seconds to recognize him. I saw an unknown face, barely a face. Then there was his hand like a fat worm in my hand. I dropped it almost immediately and the arm fell back flabbily.

There are a great number of suspicious noises in the streets, too. . . .[1]

Hallucinations? Perhaps. Roquentin first thinks this is

the explanation, as he knows his imagination is active, and he realizes that complete solitude may be detrimental to a temperament such as his. But on second thought he has dismissed this possibility. No, the malady is not in him. It is in the objects; it is inherent in them.

Until then he has believed—like everyone else—that one could use objects, handle them as one pleased, that they were useful and no more. Now he knows by experience that, just like living beings, they can become threatening. And this is true of the most common ones, a fork or a knife for instance, and even of other utterly insignificant ones.

Roquentin had developed the peculiar habit of picking up and even carrying to his mouth anything that may be lying about on the ground: chestnuts, bits of paper, old rags, and all sorts of similar dirty things. And now he finds he can no longer do this: the piece of paper was lying there before him, beside a puddle, a damp and soiled page torn from a school notebook. He had bent down to take it. He stayed bent down for a second and read "Dictation: The White Owl," but then straightened up empty-handed. It was the very same thing as with the pebble.

You want to touch objects, and it is they who touch you; they resist and push you away. They are like repugnant elements or filthy animals. They make you feel sick.

It would not be so bad if only they were honest about it. But no, they are so sneaky in their attacks. They are so treacherous. They put on a nice familiar face and then suddenly, for no apparent reason, they become aggressive —intermittently, at random, as though they decided of it themselves. So that the menace is always there, and fear together with it; even if nothing does actually happen, like that day when a real panic took hold.

I didn't know where I was going. I ran along the docks, turned into the deserted streets in the Beauvoisin district; the houses watched my flight with their mournful eyes. I repeated with anguish: Where shall I go? Where shall I go? *Anything* can happen. Sometimes, my heart pounding, I made a sudden right-about-turn: what was happening behind my back? Maybe it would start behind me and when I would turn around, suddenly, it would be too late. As long as I could stare at things nothing would happen: I looked at them as much as I could, pavements, houses, gas-lights.[2]

Nothing does happen, but how could he have known, and where could he turn for shelter? For a while Roquentin feels safe in the bright and noisy atmosphere of the cafés. There at least he thinks he need not be afraid; but this, too, is an illusion. He knows it now.

He comes into the "Railwaymen's Rendezvous" where Adolphe is at the bar. As usual some customers are playing cards, and the waitress asks the ritual question: "What will you have, Monsieur Antoine?" And at this very moment, Nausea, filthy, slimy Nausea seizes him once more. Everything becomes unbearable, especially Adolphe's suspenders, those faded purple suspenders which can hardly be seen against his blue shirt, and which, with sheep-like stubbornness, seem to want to become purple but stopped somewhere along the way without giving up their pretensions.

The suspenders, the shirt, the wall, even the card players "that too brings on the Nausea. The Nausea is not inside me: I feel it *out there* in the wall, in the suspenders, everywhere around me. It makes itself one with the café, I am the one who is within *it*."[3] What can I do but go out into the night and the cold, with the same nagging question always on my mind: Why this Nausea, and this unbearable hostility of things?

Face to Face with Existence

Today things are at their worst, and Antoine Roquentin can stand it no longer. He feels he is going out of his mind. He jumps out of the tramway on which he is riding. There is a gate before him. He pushes it open, enters into the public park, and drops onto a bench "between great black tree-trunks, between the black knotty hands reaching towards the sky." And suddenly the veil is torn away, what he was awaiting for weeks is revealed, he *sees* at last.

It left me breathless. Never, until these last few days, had I understood the meaning of 'existence.' I was like the others, like the ones walking along the seashore, all dressed in their spring finery. I said, like them, 'The ocean *is* green; that white speck up there *is* a seagull,' but I didn't feel that it existed or that the seagull was an 'existing seagull'; usually existence hides itself. It is there, around us, in us, it is *us*, you can't say two words without mentioning it, but you can never touch it. When I believed I was thinking about it, I must believe I was thinking of nothing, my head was empty, or there was just one word in my head, the word 'to be.'

Or else I was thinking . . . how can I explain it? I was thinking of *belonging*. I was telling myself that the sea belonged to the class of green objects, or that the green was a part of the quality of the sea. Even when I looked at things, I was miles from dreaming that they existed: they looked like scenery to me. I picked them up in my hands, they served me as tools, I foresaw their resistance. But that all happened on the surface. If anyone had asked me what existence was, I would have answered, in good faith, that it was nothing, simply an empty form which was added to external things without changing anything in their nature. And then all of a sudden, there it was, clear as day: existence had suddenly unveiled itself.[4]

Everything is clear now to Antoine Roquentin. As long as we live on the surface, we are content to classify objects and to use them; there is no mystery, no uneasiness. We go freely among the objects surrounding us. They help us and they are reassuring. Each one has its purpose—the doorknob is to open the door, my glass is to be filled with beer, my pipe is to be filled with tobacco. It is a clear and ordered world, the world of explanations and reasons, similar to that of mathematics, where the mind can dwell in comfort: a familiar world in which we feel at home.

But should the screen collapse and should words vanish, and with them the significance of things and their methods of use, we will see the shining velvety scales explode all around us and existence will appear heavy and pervasive. It bears down on us with all its "weight." For it is not something which allows itself to be thought of from a distance, it must weigh heavily on our heart like a great motionless beast—or else there is nothing at all.

Existence is reality showing its real face. There are no longer roots, park gates, benches or lawns, but grotesque, headstrong, and gigantic masses. The sea of the poets, the sea which sings the praise of the Lord and delights the artist, this sea does not exist. What does exist is the sea crawling under this green film, the true sea, "cold and black, full of animals," rumbling and terrifying.

And this happens for everything when the scenery col-

lapses. Even the seat on which I am sitting is now transformed into an "enormous belly turned upward, bleeding,
inflated—bloated with all its dead paws. . . . It could just
as well be a dead donkey tossed about in the water, float-
ing with the current, belly in the air in a great grey river,
a river of floods."

And my face, the object of such care and privileges,
what is it to deserve such attentions? In fact, it is nothing
but a piece of wood, a splinter of stone, neither beautiful
nor ugly, a thing "on the fringe of the vegetable world, at
the level of jelly fish," a sort of "geological embossed map."

Everything Is Absurd

Thus, when objects remove their mask, when they lose
their purpose and their use, withdrawing from the hand
of man to become themselves once more, I can only say
that they surround me. They are "beneath me, behind me,
above me. They demand nothing, they impose nothing,
they are there"—there and "de trop," bursting through
their frames and beyond all measure. The park, the chest-
nut tree and the Vellada are "de trop," and so are colors,
tastes, and smells, which are never themselves, nothing
but themselves: the simplest, most indecomposable quality has too much content in its heart; it is suspicious.

Everything is "de trop," including me: my body with
"this warm obesity which turns lazily, as if someone were
stirring it with a spoon," my face with its "crevasses and
mole holes," my hand with its fat belly and its fingers like
paws, my tongue and the water bubbling in my mouth,
even those thoughts which are born behind my head,
which come forward, stretch out and leave a funny taste
in my mouth.

And I—soft, weak, obscene, digesting, juggling with dismal thoughts—I, too, was *in the way*. . . . We were a heap of living creatures, irritated, embarrassed at ourselves, we hadn't the slightest reason to be there, none of us, each one, confused, vaguely alarmed, felt in the way in relation to the others.[5]

"In the way," writes Sartre; that is, without explanation or reason. We are in the realm of the absurd. For this is absurdity, true absurdity. It is true that we often speak of absurdity in connection with something that was said or done, but we sense then how fragile our judgment is, and that it might be thrown back at us.

A disorganized movement which does not fit in with our habits, or incoherent words which are not within the grasp of our logic are often said to be absurd. But we need only change our perspective to see the madman's ravings in relation to his delirium and the gesture of the primitive man in relation to the prelogical mentality behind it. The madman has changed sides, whereas here there is no way out; absurdity is in relation to nothing. Whichever way you try to look at things, it is still there. It is fundamental, it is absolute. This root gives me the impression of "unwinding itself a little, denying its existence to lose itself in a frenzied excess," and there is nothing in relation to which it is not absurd.

Of course, I could have seen the seed sprout and the tree grow; I could also know many things about the nature of this root and its function, and this would allow me to display my knowledge of science. But this is not the point. By seeking refuge in science, I would have left the world of existence. I would be dealing with a certain root, a well-classified root, the idea of a root, but not with "that," with the "hard and compact skin of a sea lion," this "oily, callous, headstrong" thing. That is below all explanation. We spoke of absurdity; we might as well have said contingency. "To exist is simply *to be there;* those who exist let themselves be encountered, but you cannot deduce anything from them."[6] They are gratuitous, unjustifiable.

It is obviously difficult to bury oneself in such a feeling, which upsets us so much when we become conscious of it, and it is understandable that philosophers tried to overcome this contingency by resorting to a necessary self-causal being. But such a being is pure invention and but an illusory escape. "No necessary being can explain existence: contingency is not a delusion, a probability which can be dissipated; it is the absolute, consequently, the perfect free gift."[7] One cannot modify being at will.

And thus Antoine Roquentin wrote down his thoughts as his journal progressed. Is this but the fruit of the author's imagination or the sober talk of a philosopher? There may have been some debate on this point, but the answer is quite clear to us. Throughout the pages of Roquentin's journal it is the philosopher who is searching within himself and who suddenly yields to the obvious, for this Nausea is not a figment of the imagination, but an experience, a metaphysical experience. The language and the tone of this novel dismiss the possibility of a mere game. It is all too sincere.

Sartre is in the presence of being. The intuition which makes the philosopher may be granted him in many ways, the essential is that it is granted. Here it is through a harrowing experience, both disgusting and frightening, that being is grasped in its contingency and its gratuity, but the starting point of Sartre's thought (for we are no longer dealing with Roquentin, but with Sartre himself) has been fixed and so conceptualization is now possible. Indeed it has already begun and will be continued throughout *Being and Nothingness.*

The Refusal of Traditional Concepts

Sartre first warns us, and this is of the utmost importance, that he most definitely fits into a tradition. "Modern thought," he tells us, "has realized considerable progress by reducing the existent to the series of appearances which manifest it."[8]

According to Roger Verneaux, this means something like the following: Hume was right to eliminate metaphysical entities and to lay the foundations of an experimental philosophy. Kant was right when he restricted the sphere of possible knowledge to phenomena. Comte was right in proclaiming the advent of the positivistic era and the abolition of the metaphysical era. Renouvoir was right to adopt "the point of view of Knowledge." Lachelier, Brunschvicg, Hamelin were all right to reject Kant's "Thing-in-itself." And Husserl, above all, was right to accept only the pure phenomenon as apodictic and unquestionable, and so was Heidegger when he refused to make a distinction between phenomenon and being.[9]

However things may stand with this philosophical tradition and whatever the exact contribution of each philosopher to the evolution of thought, one thing is certain: Sartre's ontology satisfies modern requirements and dwells upon phenomena while it never discusses substance, nor potency, nor even essence in the usual sense of the word. These concepts are now thoroughly obsolete. Tied up with a metaphysics that has lost all validity, they have collapsed with it.

Sartre gives us his views on the subject. Concerning substance, he writes:

> There is no longer an exterior for the existent if one means by that a superficial covering which hides from sight the true nature of the object. And this true nature in turn, if it is to be the secret reality of the thing, which one can have a presentiment of or which one can suppose but can never reach because it is the 'interior' of the object under consideration—this nature no longer exists. The appearances which manifest the existent are neither interior nor exterior; they are all equal, they all refer to other appearances, and none of them is privileged. Force, for example, is not a metaphysical conatus of an unknown kind which hides behind its effects (accelerations, deviations, etc.); it is the totality of these effects. Similarly an electric current does not have a secret reverse side; it is nothing but the totality of the physical-chemical actions which manifest it.[10]

We must therefore forget the concept of substance, and together with it, that of potency. The famous distinction between potency and act, so dear to Aristotle and his followers, is utterly pointless. It corresponds to nothing. It is not always easy to accept this, so cumbersome are our habits of thought. For example, we find it difficult not to consider genius as "a particular capacity to produce certain works, which was not exhausted exactly in producing them."[11] Genius would or would not find its true expression, but it would in any case be distinct from the produced works and would surpass them. As one of our critics once so humorously said about a famous writer:

"He does not burden us with great works and he is ranked high more because of what he is capable of doing than because of what he does." And yet this way of thinking, common though it may be, is all wrong. Man cannot be separated from his acts. He is only what they make him. Thus "the genius of Proust is neither the work considered in isolation nor the subjective ability to produce it; it is the work considered as the totality of the manifestations of the person,"[12] which means that in this field as in all others, there is no place for potency, since the act is everything.

As for essence, the term can be retained, but only with the correct meaning. It is out of the question to allow it to denote something behind appearances, something intelligible which our intelligence can grasp by disengaging it from experience. Essence is not a property sunk in the cavity of the existent. It is not behind the manifestations of something, but is rather the reason for these manifestations, their law. It is their concatenation and of the same order as them. It is therefore also itself an appearance. Thus there is nothing behind phenomena, and we must dismiss all metaphysical "entities." Nietzsche had violently denounced "the illusion of worlds-behind-the-scene" —Sartre feels nothing can be added to this: the condemnation was final.

But the consequences might be serious indeed. This reality reduced to appearances might well be nothing but a mirage and have no other existence than that bestowed upon it by our mind. We would then have to go back to Berkeley's *Esse est percipi*. And this is what the modern idealists thought, for whom phenomena exist only to the extent that they are representations; that is, as objects of thought. The collapse of the worlds-behind-the-scene led to the collapse of the world itself. Outside of thought, there is nothing. But Sartre does not allow himself to be convinced on this especially important point. Rejecting both idealism and the old realism, he goes beyond them.

Beyond Idealism and Realism

For what of the desk on which I am writing? Is it a mere representation? Most certainly not: my desk exists, with the clutter of papers and books on it, with my tobacco and my lighter among them. It is there before me and it is not me, no more so than the room and its furnishings.

If it were only thought, the principle binding the series of its representations and making it what it is would be dependent on my whims, and this is not the case. The object depends neither on me nor on anyone. It is I who depend on it. It binds me and resists me. It always surpasses the appearances which reveal it.

Unlike the image which is given once for all and can never be enriched, the object is infinite. The multiple aspects under which it appears do not exhaust its richness. It is an infinity of others which do not appear, which may never appear. Thus a perception never ceases to teach me something. Going from discovery to discovery, it puts me in front of an inexhaustible, in front of an infinite series of representations, so that the object is altogether *in* the representation I have of it, and at the same time altogether *outside* it.

This is the way it has to be, for what the idealist did not see is that the disappearance of the object would be the disappearance of thought. Since Husserl, we know what knowledge is, and above all what it is not. The person who knows is not (as was believed and taught by such men as Brunschvicg, Lalande or Meyerson) a sort of machine for blending and building, a sort of spider which, after drawing its victims to its web would coat them with spittle and slowly swallow them, reducing them to its own substance, so that the table I touch, the house I see, the rock I am climbing would finally be nothing but a well-ordered array of contents of consciousness.

No, this is not knowledge. It is neither a sort of digestion, nor a series of complex transformations, nor a subtle construction game. It is not a sleight of hand.

To know is to "burst out toward." It is for example "to wrench away from my moist gastric intimity to fly over there, beyond myself, near the tree and yet outside it, for it escapes me and casts me off and I can no more lose myself in it than it can become diluted in me. Outside of it, outside of me."[13] In other words, to know is to aim, to aim at an object. And it is in this sense that Husserl says that knowledge is "intentional."

But knowledge is only one of the possible forms of consciousness. I can have a representation of the tree, but I can also love it, fear it, or hate it. In all cases, there is a surpassing and an intentionality:

> "To hate someone is another way of bursting out toward him, it is to find oneself suddenly in the presence of a stranger for which we first live, we first endure his objective quality of being 'hateful.' All of a sudden these famous subjective reactions—hate, fear, fondness—are but ways to discover *the world*. It is things which suddenly reveal themselves to us as hateful, likable, horrible, lovable."[14]

Consciousness therefore always bursts out toward an object, an object which we know does not and cannot come from it. It is impossible for the subjective to give rise to the objective, for the immanent to give rise to the transcendent, for nonbeing to produce being. It must therefore be that the object exists when thought is revealing it. Without it, there would be neither knowledge nor consciousness.

To reject the metaphysical realities of realism and Kant's Thing-in-itself is not to consent to the annihilation of thought. It may be true that only phenomena exist, but the being of the phenomenon does not exist only to the extent that it appears. It is this infinite which founds all its manifestations and constantly surpasses them. "The transphenomenal being of phenomena" says Sartre.

And ontology takes on a new meaning: since it cannot go beyond the phenomenon, its purpose is to describe and not to explain. It is phenomenological.

The In-Itself

But when we are dealing with the transphenomenal being of the phenomenon, ontology soon becomes inadequate. What can be said about the being revealed to us in *Nausea?* One might clarify statements and avoid misinterpretation, but it does not seem that much more can be done.

First we must discard the error which holds that being is created. God, according to theologians and quite a few philosophers too, would have made the world out of nothing. This is how they explain the emergence of the world. One: The created being will be dependent of its creator, immanent to divine consciousness, a mode of this consciousness. But then there can be no objective existence. We said, on the subject of idealism, that we cannot build the objective with the subjective; and this argument is valid here too. One cannot make being out of consciousness, even divine consciousness.

Or else, if one is willing to accept the impossible, creation would be this fulguration of which Leibniz speaks, and the created being would be set by God over against Himself, outside His consciousness. But then it would be its own support, its own foundation and would consequently be cut away from the Creator. "Even if it had been created, being-in-itself would be *inexplicable* in terms of creation; for it assumes its being beyond the creation."[15]

And thus the hypothesis of creation is of no use in either case; it explains nothing. Either being is independent of God, or it does not exist. Does this mean that it creates itself? Certainly not. For being to be *causa sui* would suppose that it is prior to itself, which is out of the question. It follows that the only acceptable affirmation is that being is; it is its own support, it is itself.

It is neither active nor passive as some would have it. These concepts are meaningful only in relation to human conduct. Man alone can be active since he uses means to reach the end he has in mind. And neither is passivity a characteristic of the object. It is our way of interpreting the resistance of things. Now this resistance is a response to our projects. Without them, it would not exist. "The self-consistency of being is beyond the active as it is beyond the passive."

It is also beyond affirmation and negation, which both presuppose the distinction between subject and object.

"Affirmation is always affirmation of something; that is, the act of affirming is distinguished from the thing affirmed. But if we suppose an affirmation in which the affirmed comes to fulfill the affirming and is confused with it, this affirmation can not be affirmed—owing to too much of plenitude."[16] Now this is the case for being, about which we cannot even speak of immanence, since immanence is still a sort of connection with itself.

Thus being appears as "an immanence which cannot realize itself, an affirmation which cannot affirm itself, an activity which cannot act."[17] Glued to itself, opaque, solid, full of itself and without secrets, it has neither within nor without. It is not related, it cannot enter into any connections without anything. It is therefore isolated and also motionless: beyond becoming and beyond time. "It is itself indefinitely and it exhausts itself in being. . . . It is, and when it gives way, one cannot even say that it no longer is. . . . The full positivity of being is re-formed on its giving way. It was and at present other beings are: that is all."[18]

It is therefore clear that it cannot be derived from anything, neither from the necessary, nor from the possible, nor from another existent. Necessity maintains us in an ideal world, like that of mathematics. The possible can be understood only in terms of consciousness. As for deriving being from another being, this would suppose in the latter an activity of which we know it is not capable.

Only one conclusion is possible: there is no reason for being, no cause, no explanation. It simply is, realizing identity in its strongest form; it is itself or, to quote from *Nausea,* it is contingent, absurd, "de trop"—"de trop" for all eternity.

NOTES

1. Jean-Paul Sartre, *Nausea* (New York: New Directions, 1964), p. 11.
2. *Ibid.*, p. 107–108.
3. *Ibid.*, p. 31.
4. *Ibid.*, p. 171.
5. *Ibid.*, p. 172–173.
6. *Ibid.*, p. 176.
7. *Ibid.*, p. 176.
8. Jean-Paul Sartre, *Being and Nothingness* (New York: Citadel Press, 1966), p. xlv.
9. Roger Verneaux, *Leçons sur l'Existentialisme,* 1st ed., Cours et documents de philosophie (Paris, 1949), p. 114.
10. Sartre, *op. cit.,* p. xlv.
11. *Ibid.*, p. xlvi.
12. *Ibid.*, p. xlvi.
13. Jean-Paul Sartre, *Situations I* (Paris: Gallimard, 1947), p. 32.
14. *Ibid.*, p. 34.
15. Sartre, *Being and Nothingness,* p. lxiv.
16. *Ibid.*, p. lxv.
17. *Ibid.*, p. lxv.
18. *Ibid.*, p. lxvi.

(II)

Consciousness and Nothingness

Being, in whose presence we have been led by Nausea reveals itself as opaque and solid. It is in itself. It is itself; this is how our intuition presents it to us. Deduction and reasoning do not change it in any way. And how could they, since they are only instruments which lead to intuition and since all knowledge is intuitive?[1]

But the being thus represented does not encompass the whole of being. Facing the in-itself which made him feel nauseous there is Roquentin, living his harrowing experience. There is the object, but there is also man—man whom no one can say is of the same substance as the object, since he is consciousness. Consciousness, says Sartre, exists like a tree, like a blade of grass. "It dilutes, scatters itself, tries to lose itself on the brown wall, along the lamp-post or down there in the evening mist." It may even try to forget itself. "But it *never* forgets itself." It is consciousness of being a consciousness forgetting itself. "There is a stifled voice which tells it: 'The train leaves in two hours,' and there is the consciousness of this voice. There is also consciousness of a face. . . . There is a consciousness of this body walking slowly in a dark street."[2]

Knowledge of man is therefore knowledge of consciousness. And ontology must turn in this direction; an ontology which will throw light upon ourselves and upon our destiny.

Interrogation

For what are we? Our investigation may be long and arduous, but the essential is to know how to tackle the problem. One might be tempted—and we must immediately say this would be a great mistake—to try to reach consciousness in itself, isolated from everything, allowing ourselves to perform an unjustifiable abstraction. We already know that consciousness is always consciousness of something and that it can therefore not be separated from being.

This amounts to saying that in the true sense of the word, man is not. The only concrete reality is that of man within the world. One might possibly conceive of the in-itself independently of consciousness, but it is impossible to think of consciousness independently of the in-itself. So if man is ever to reveal his mystery, it will not be through introspection (which never got us anywhere), but through his relations with being, through his attitudes and his conduct.

His patterns of conduct are plentiful, however. And here again we must make a choice. Now, in Sartre's view, only one choice is possible: interrogation. "This man that *I am*—if I apprehend him such as he is at this moment in the world, I establish that he stands before being in an attitude of interrogation."[3]

And it is indeed true that man, in his curiosity and in

his anguish, is always asking questions. He wants to know; he questions another being "about its ways of being and about its being." But what does this mean? It certainly means that the questioner does not know that he will get an answer, an answer that may be negative, but—even if it is affirmative—will be formulated as "It is thus and not otherwise," so that every question presupposes both our ignorance and the possibility of nonbeing.

> The permanent possibility of nonbeing, outside us and within, conditions our questions about being. Furthermore it is nonbeing which is going to limit the reply. What being *will be* must of necessity arise on the basis of what *it is not*. Whatever being is, it will allow this formulation: Being is *that*, and outside of that, *nothing*![4]

We recall Roquentin's anguished surprise when, overwhelmed by existence, he saw himself surrounded with abundance, an abundance of which he could not rid himself. Existence was everywhere, to infinity, with no other form but itself. "Everywhere blossomings, hatchings out, my ears buzzed with existence, my very flesh throbbed and opened, abandoned itself to the universal burgeoning. It was repugnant."[5] And now it is nonbeing which is revealing itself through interrogation, closing in on all sides. Now all is wrapped "by a mantle of nothingness."

Man is the being who asks himself questions. And for the same reason, man is the being to whom nothingness reveals itself. Indeed, negation refers us to nonbeing, but affirmation is of importance, too. It goes against most philosophers' thinking, but then Sartre is not satisfied to affirm the essential foundation of his thoughts—he is trying to prove it.

For the philosopher, negation is but a category of the spirit, a quality of judgment. The synthesis characterizing the latter "is here brought about by means of the copula being," and there by means of the copula "nonbeing." Likewise, the manual operation of separating and the manual operation of uniting are two actions possessing the reality of fact. Thus negation would be "at the end" [*au bout*] of the judicative act but not "in the being."[6] Negation would amount to affirmation, the same act being to assert that something is not, as to deny that something is. Philosophers' opinion, yes; but not reason—at least this is what Sartre thinks.

Negation and Nonbeing

First, it is not true to state that negation is inseparable from judgment and therefore always at the end of the judicative act, no more than interrogation. Often, no doubt, the question takes the form of a judgment, and the interrogator answers according to the ordinary rules of the discourse, that it is a logically construed proposition. But question and reply can also be formulated quite differently. One can question by a look, by a gesture, and moreover one is not necessarily addressing a person.

The driver examining the engine of his stalled car and the watchmaker scrutinizing the various mechanisms of a watch, are in fact patiently asking a question. They expect an answer, that which the engine and the watch will give them through a disclosure of being or nonbeing. To the mechanic, for instance, the carburetor reveals either that there is something there or that there is nothing there. And in the case of a negative judgment, it is this nothing which precedes negation and justifies it. "The necessary condition for our saying *not* is that nonbeing be a perpetual presence in us and outside of us, that nothingness haunt being."[7]

This may sound surprising, but the description of a common experience provides a striking illustration.

> I have an appointment with Pierre at four o'clock. I arrive at the café a quarter of an hour late. Pierre is always punctual. Will he have waited for me? I look at the room, the patrons, and I say, 'He is not here.' Is there an intuition of Pierre's absence, or does negation indeed enter in only with judgment? At first sight it seems absurd to speak here of intuition since to be exact there could not be an intuition of *nothing* and since the absence of Pierre is this nothing. Popular consciousness, however, bears witness to this intuition. Do we not say, for example, 'I suddenly saw that he was not there.' Is this just a matter of misplacing the negation? Let us look at it a little closer.[8]

What is actually happening in me and around me when, entering the café in search of Pierre, I look around the room? Unquestionably the objects, and most of all the faces of those in the café are disappearing one after the other. This would not be the case, of course, should I suddenly discover Pierre. The whole café would then organize around him. But Pierre is not there.

> This does not mean that I discover his absence in some precise spot in the establishment. In fact Pierre is absent from the *whole* café; his absence fixes the café in its evanescence; the café remains *ground*; it persists in offering itself as an undifferentiated totality to my only marginal attention; it slips into the background; it pursues its nihilation. Only it makes itself ground for a

determined figure; it carries the figure everywhere in front of it, presents the figure everywhere to me. This figure which slips constantly between my look and the solid, real objects of the café is precisely a perpetual disappearance; it is Pierre raising himself as nothingness on the ground of the nihilation of the café. So that what is offered to intuition is a flickering of nothingness; it is the nothingness of the ground, the nihilation of which summons and demands the appearance of the figure, and it is the figure—the nothingness which slips as a *nothing* to the surface of the ground. It serves as foundation for the judgment—'Pierre is not here.' It is in fact the intuitive apprehension of a double nihilation.[9]

And thus the café is there before me. It is there in its reality, in its fullness of being. It is there with its tables, its booths, and its mirrors, with its patrons and its smoky atmosphere, with the sound of voices, footsteps and rattling saucers, yet I only need to be searching for Pierre for nothingness to appear, in a confusion of form and content.

However, this nothingness which experience reveals to us is not, as Hegel thought, one of the components of the real. For being and nonbeing are not two complementary components—like dark and light—two empty abstractions: thesis and antithesis whose reunion alone would be at the basis of concrete realities.[10] Neither is it the infinite milieu evoked by Heidegger, from which being would emerge and in which it would remain suspended.

No this is not nothingness. It can be conceived "neither outside of being nor as a complementary, abstract notion, nor as an infinite milieu." It is at the heart of Being, coiled up like a worm. It inhabits these "realities which are not only objects of judgment, but which are experienced, opposed, feared," and can be called *négatités*. Thus "distance, absence, change, otherness, repulsion, regret, distraction etc." are swarming with "beings which possess as much reality and efficacy as other beings, but which enclose within themselves nonbeing."[11]

And this is how it must be, since Nothingness has only a borrowed existence: It is from Being that it draws its being, so that the annihilation of everything would not be, as is commonly thought, the advent of nonbeing, but rather its disappearance.

We can rely on language on this point which is significant: words have definite meanings which govern their use. Thus we make a distinction between "nothing" and "nobody." The being that is negated is clearly specified. And it always is. When a child is told "Touch nothing," the meaning is quite clear. The child knows that he must not touch any of the papers, the books, or other objects he might damage. Similarly, when we say "I know nothing," we mean that we know nothing concerning those things about which we are being questioned—unless we happen to be dealing with Socrates, for whom nothingness is "the totality of being considered as Truth."

Thus, in all cases, nothingness appears only on the surface of being, it is supported by being, as it were. But this tells us nothing of its origin. We must search further; a search which will greatly increase our knowledge of man.

Being is In-itself. It is full positivity; it has nothing to do with nothingness. And as for nothingness, since it is not, it obviously cannot derive from itself the necessary force to "nihilate itself." We must therefore either leave the question unanswered, or find something else. And this something else might well be consciousness. Man, before whom nothingness unveils itself, would then be the being by which nothingness comes to the world. This is the only hypothesis left, and we will now examine it.

Emotive and Imaginative Consciousness

To simplify our task and see things more clearly, it seems a good idea to turn to Sartre's psychological descriptions of emotive and imaginative consciousness in his *Sketch for a Theory of Emotions* and *The Psychology of Imagination*. Psychologists have said a great deal about emotion, but two names stand out above all others: William James and Pierre Janet.

For William James, emotion is merely the awareness of organic disturbances. The physiological changes follow immediately upon the perception of the excitant and our consciousness of these modifications, as they are taking place, is emotion. In other words, we are sad because we are crying, afraid because we are shaking, angry because we are hitting someone.[12]

For Pierre Janet, on the contrary, emotion appears as a behavior—but a behavior of defeat. The phenomena occur when a living and conscious being is suddenly exposed to a modification of his physical, and most of all, of the social milieu in which he is immersed, if he has not been prepared by a prior education to adapt to it automatically, and if he has not the strength or the time necessary to adapt to them at the present moment. There is, then, an uncoordinated nervous expenditure which brings about exhaustion.[13]

But Sartre disagrees with both James and Janet. If a ferocious beast, escaped from its menagerie, should find me in its path and I am utterly deprived of all means of defense, it is true that my legs give way under me, my heart begins to thump, and I turn pale. It is true that I might even faint, though this is apparently the most stupid conduct I could adopt, the worst adapted to danger since I am doing quite the opposite of what I should. Because I am frightened, I yield to danger.

Is this merely a matter of pure organic disturbances or even the rout of a surprised mind—at least as Janet describes it, with a lack of precision which seems to relate it to automatism? If we look closer, we see that this is not the case. It is an attitude of consciousness which expresses an attempt to escape, for fainting away is a refuge. To be sure, I acted without calculation or reflection, but "the urgency of the danger was the motive for this attempt to annihilate it, which called for magical behavior." In my desire to escape from the danger, I tried to annihilate it, I refused it, I denied it. I behaved as an ostrich would. It may not help me very much, but that is not the point. This does not affect my intention.

And the same is true of all emotions. Here we have the man in danger who faints of fear—there the patient (Pierre Janet's patient for instance) who, in her desire to avoid a painful confession, throws a fit of nerves in front of her doctor. Elsewhere, one shouts for joy at hearing some good news, or, after a hard blow, one seeks shelter in an attitude of dejection. But it is always the same attempt at escape. The patient escapes by means of her nervous crisis from a situation which requires an effort, the oversensitive student uses his tears to avoid the questions of the examiner, while the student who finds he has been successful sings and dances to escape the hostile circumstances which, at that very moment, are threatening a joy he wishes to preserve. As for the man who has just learned that he is ruined, he too escapes from a universe over which he no longer has any hold. He settles in melancholy. He "lowers the flame of life to a pin-point." In all cases, we have the desire to adapt, but in a magical manner. One escapes danger and risk not by facing them, but by trying to eliminate what has not been avoidable.

We can therefore see consciousness in action in our emotions, but we could see it just as well in our imagination. Imagination is also a form of magical activity. It too makes light of all difficulties. It is a sort of "incantation destined to produce the object of one's thought, the thing one desires, in a manner that one can take possession of it."[14]

As with emotion, the true nature of imagination has often been misunderstood. It was generally believed that the image was a sort of thing or object, existing in consciousness as the content in its container, or, if one prefers, as a painting in a museum.

But this is not the image. In that sense, one could even say that it does not exist. What does exist is imagination; imagination which is also an attitude of consciousness, a behavior. The image of Pierre is Pierre whom I see: his eyes, his face, his build, his general appearance, at a given time and in a given place; that is, the intuition of Pierre. Yes, but it is the intuition of one who is absent: Pierre is far away, he may even be dead, and those features through which I reach him threaten dissolution. In any case he is not there, which means that while I am conscious of him, I am also conscious of his present nothingness, or more simply that he is as nonbeing. And this impression will be all the stronger as I am thinking of a person I love and whom I am missing. It can also happen that I yield to dreams, that I dream of Pierre. He then appears to me as nonexisting, as existing elsewhere. It is the world, on the contrary, which recedes or disappears. "Imagination is the great unrealizing function of consciousness."

> To posit an image is to construct an object on the fringe of the whole of reality, which means therefore to hold the real at a distance, to free oneself from it, in a word, to deny it. Or, in other words, to deny that an object belongs to the real is to deny the real in positing the object; the two negations are complementary, the former being the condition for the latter.[15]

Imagination therefore, as well as emotion, brings us face to face with negation, with refusal. In both cases, being is put out of circuit—or rather, so it seems. But the most cursory examination will show that this is not at all the case. The beast that was terrifying me did not vanish when I fainted, and denying the real did not make it fade away. Putting being out of circuit can be no more nor less than putting consciousness out of circuit.

Human reality can annihilate nothing in being. One might say that it has a hold only upon itself. What does change is simply its relation with things. It is human reality alone which is receding, escaping, annihilating itself. It sets itself out of reach by retiring beyond a nothingness, and not only when man is feeling or dreaming, but in all the manifestations of its activity. Endlessly, it breaks away and falls off. I am not the scenery I am admiring, nor the man I apprehend. I burst out toward the world, but without ever coinciding with it, without losing msyelf in it. It is but an illusion fit for poets and mystics to want to identify with nature. And besides, what for? There would then be no more knowledge since one can affirm something only on condition that one is not that thing. There would be no more consciousness.

Even when Roquentin is overwhelmed by existence and he is caught in the "swooning abundance" of things, in the suspicious and the viscous, even then, as we have seen, consciousness does not forget itself; to forget would be its downfall. Between man and the world, there is therefore always a break, a nothing—this nothing which is brought on by the presence of man and which isolates him from everything.

Consciousness Is Nothingness

But if it is in the nature of consciousness to constantly draw back beyond a nothingness, is it not because it is itself a nothingness?

We follow Mathieu—the philosopher in *The Roads to Freedom*—as he is walking along the Seine. "Outside. Everything is outside: the trees on the quay, the two houses by the bridge that lend a pink flush to the darkness, the petrified gallop of Henry IV above my head—solid objects all of them. Inside: nothing. . . . Myself: nothing."[16] There is certainly nothing very philosophical about this, but neither should we think that it can be ascribed to a delirious imagination. It expresses in its own way the nonbeing of consciousness. "The being by which Nothingness comes to the world must be its own Nothingness." And so it is.

All consciousness is consciousness of something, but it is also and simultaneously consciousness of self. It is impossible to conceive of a perception, a feeling, a desire, a will which would not be conscious. One does not think the absurd.

We must be clear however. This is true only if we do not confuse consciousness and knowledge, as is often done. "To know is to know that one knows," said Alain. And this was a mistake, a serious mistake. To be conscious of knowing, is not knowing; no more than to be conscious of counting means that I know myself as counting. Similarly, when I perceive something, I know but I do not know *myself*.

It is true that it can happen—and it happens very often indeed—that one observes oneself, that one examines and judges oneself, but this is another matter. We are no longer dealing with immediate consciousness, but with reflection. And the latter, with the duality it implies, is possible only if immediate consciousness exists.

Besides, to claim otherwise and define consciousness as self-knowledge would only lead to an inextricable dead-end. Let us try it.

> If we accept the law of the knower-known dyad, then a third term will be necessary in order for the knower to become known in turn, and we will be faced with this dilemma: Either we stop at any one term of the series—the known, the knower known, the knower known by the knower, etc. In this case the totality of the phenomenon falls into the unknown; that is, we always bump up against a non-self-conscious reflection and a final term. Or else we affirm the necessity of an infinite regress (*idea ideae ideae*, etc.), which is absurd.[17]

We must choose between an endless series of steps or an

arbitrary stop, and consciousness is escaping us in both cases. We must therefore admit that though he is involved in all knowledge, the subject is not himself an object of knowledge and that to reduce him to this status would be to destroy him. Before Descartes' reflective *cogito* "I think that I think," there is a prereflective *cogito* without which it could not exist.

But it is not easy to discuss these matters; we all agree that one should not identify knowledge and consciousness. But what can we say about consciousness itself? There is little choice. It seems we will have to use Sartre's own words: "Consciousness of self is not dual," he tells us. It is an "immediate relation of the self to itself." Or again, "Every positional consciousness of an object is at the same time a non-positional consciousness of itself." And even in this form, statements are ambiguous. They might create the very confusion we are trying to avoid: "We can no longer use this expression in which the 'of self' still evokes the idea of knowledge. (Henceforth we shall put the 'of' inside parentheses to show that it merely satisfies a grammatical requirement.)[18]

> This self-consciousness we ought to consider not as a new consciousness, but as *the only mode of existence which is possible for a consciousness of something*. Just as an extended object is compelled to exist according to three dimensions, so an intention, a pleasure, a grief can exist only as immediate self-consciousness. If the intention is not a thing in consciousness, then the being of the intention can be only consciousness.[19]

But we must go even further. It may be true that immediate primitive consciousness is not a useless search

of the subject after himself; it is not this reflection which
implies an unsurmountable duality, but neither is it coincidence with self. The object, as we have seen, is what it
is—opaque and solid, identical to itself. The table on
which I am writing is this table and no other. And it is
fully this table. The same is true of all things around me.
We are here in the realm of identity. But it is quite a
different matter for consciousness.

Take belief, for instance. It is consciousness (of) belief
or it would not be. But we do not have on the one hand
my belief and on the other my consciousness, of which I
could claim that each one is what it is, as I could claim
of any object. We are dealing here with two different
terms; my consciousness is not my belief and yet they are
inseparable. They constantly refer to one another, they
blend into one another. "Consciousness (of) belief is belief and belief is consciousness (of) belief."[20] It is impossible to get away from it. The principle of identity is
valid only within the region of being, it is not valid for
consciousness.[21] The latter does not coincide with itself.
It is not itself, it is presence to self. With respect to the
plenitude of the thing, it is decompression, ungluing, it
is (so to speak) a malady of being. Imagine, as Gabriel
Marcel suggests, two sheets of paper stuck together. They
may coincide perfectly, but it is possible that there is a
slight space between them. And this space appears as less-
being with respect to perfect coincidence.

But this is only an image, which would lead us into
error if it were taken literally. For if consciousness is separated from itself, it is nothing which separates it. "Ordinarily what separates is a distance in space, a lapse of time,
a psychological difference, or simply the individuality of

two co-presents—in short a qualified reality."[22] There is nothing like that here; the separation of which we must speak in connection with consciousness is but its impossibility to coincide with itself.

And this is nothingness, this impossibility, this fissure. Nothingness does not exist but is a wrenching away, a break with the being around the self and first of all with self.

The For-Itself

We were inquiring at first into the nature of consciousness. That was the true goal of our investigations. And we now have the answer. Consciousness, or human reality, is the being by which nothingness comes to the world because it is itself nothingness; or, to use one of Sartre's apparently baffling statements: "The Being by which Nothingness arrives in the world is a being such that in its being, the Nothingness of its being is in question."[23]

We are thus in the presence of subjectivity, that is, of the transphenomenal Being of the subject. In *Nausea,* we encountered the *In-itself.* Now we are dealing with the *For-itself.* We might also say that we are at grips with freedom.

For the For-itself and freedom are one and the same thing. It is because man is free that he can question himself and the world, that he can wrest himself away from himself and from the world. Sartre wrote, "Descartes, following the Stoics, has given a name to this possibility which human reality has to secrete a nothingness which isolates it—it is *freedom.*"[24]

Once more we recall Mathieu's reflections in *The Reprieve.* His thoughts vividly translate the impression each one of us should have of himself: "I am nothing; I possess nothing. As inseparable from the world as light, and yet exiled, gliding like light over the surface of stones and water, but nothing can ever grasp me or absorb me. Outside the world, outside the past, outside myself: freedom is exile, and I am condemned to be free."[25]

The mystery of man is therefore the mystery of his freedom.

NOTES

1. Jean-Paul Sartre, *Being and Nothingness* (New York: Citadel Press, 1966), p. 229.
2. Jean-Paul Sartre, *Nausea* (New York: New Directions Publishing, 1964), pp. 227–228.
3. Sartre, *Being and Nothingness*, p. 4.
4. *Ibid.*, p. 5.
5. Sartre, *Nausea*, p. 179.
6. Sartre, *Being and Nothingness*, p. 6.
7. *Ibid.*, p. 11.
8. *Ibid.*, p. 9.
9. *Ibid.*, p. 10.
10. *Ibid.*, p. 12.
11. *Ibid.*, p. 21.
12. Cf. Jean-Paul Sartre, *Sketch for a Theory of the Emotions* (London: Methuen, 1962).
13. *Ibid.*
14. Jean-Paul Sartre, *The Psychology of Imagination* (New York: Citadel Press, 1966), p. 177.
15. *Ibid.*, p. 266.
16. Jean-Paul Sartre, *The Reprieve* (New York: Knopf, 1947), p. 362.
17. Sartre, *Being and Nothingness*, p. lii. It should be noted that the phrase *idea ideae ideae* is incomplete. It should have read *idea, idea ideae, idea ideae ideae*, etc.
18. Translator's note: "Self-consciousness" will generally be used instead of "consciousness [of] self."
19. Sartre, *op. cit.*, p. liv.
20. *Ibid.*, p. 51.
21. *Ibid.*, p. 50: "The principle of identity can be said to be synthetic not only because it limits its scope to a region of definite being, but in particular because it masses within it the infinity of density. . . . Identity is the limiting concept of unification."

22. *Ibid.*, p. 53.
23. *Ibid.*, p. 23.
24. *Ibid.*, p. 24.
25. Sartre, *The Reprieve*, p. 363.

(III)

Man Is Condemned To Be Free

There is nothing very new about granting to man the privilege of freedom. Most philosophers did it. From Socrates to Bergson, many could have written these lines from *The Flies:* "The bane of gods and kings. The bitterness of knowing men are free." But this is not the important point. What really matters is not the word that is used but the reality behind it, and we must discover this reality in order to reach a clearer knowledge of consciousness: whatever we may have said so far, a mistake on the subject of freedom would be a mistake on the subject of man. We must therefore carry our inquiry further.

But, as we might expect, this will have to be done without any help from the philosophers. For what do they say?

Freedom Is Not What Philosophers Claim

On the one hand we have those who are "concerned to find cases of decision for which there exists no prior cause, or deliberations concerning two opposed acts which are equally possible and possess causes (and motives) of exactly the same weight."[1] In their view, man is free when he acts for no good reason, when it makes no difference whether he does or does not do this or that; that is, when he decides of his behavior without cause. If I open my purse and choose completely at random any one of the coins inside, I am acting freely. Others, however, claim that "there is no action without a cause and that the most insigificant gesture (raising the right hand rather than the left, etc.) refers to causes and motives which confer its meaning upon it."[2]

Freedom of indifference or acceptance of necessity: the first inclines toward chance, the latter toward determinism. Thought, as Jean Wahl would say, is wavering between Epicurus and Zeno. It would seem that the latter are closest to the truth. Every real action is "intentional." It is ruled by causes or motives, whether they be clearly formulated or merely experienced. Not indeed that every reasonable being can necessarily predict all the consequences of his actions. The emperor Constantine had not foreseen that by establishing himself at Byzantium he would be at the origin of a schism and of the weakening of the Empire. But it is necessary to "intentionally realize a conscious project." The careless smoker who negligently throws his lighted cigarette on the grass and thus starts a fire has not acted. His gesture is lacking the intention which would make it an act.

However, if those who believe in a freedom of determination are most certainly correct on this point, their conception is nonetheless inacceptable. Their analysis is not thorough enough and they only see part of the question. They do not ask whence causes derive their value in the free act and finally reduce human activity of a rigorous sequel of causes and effects. Their so-called freedom founders into determinism.

Negation on the one hand, unintelligibility on the other; freedom is still eluding us. Sartre will therefore leave classical philosophy to its problems and debates which he deems both tedious and pointless, and return to his investigation of consciousness.

He first gets rid of the common preconceived notion that will is an exceptional function. It is the voluntary act, and the voluntary act alone, which is always endowed with the privilege of freedom. Many would be free when, after deliberating, he makes a decision. It would of course be well understood that the other modes of his activity, such as emotion or passion, should be ascribed to determinism. Thus, by virtue of this strange duality, we would be dealing with a hybrid being, both free and determined, whose principal enterprise is to utilize to its own advantage the determinism governing the greatest part of its activity or, more concretely, to find the least unsatisfactory solution to the eternal conflict between will and passion.

This was the opinion already held by the Stoics—and also by Descartes, though the latter avoided this dichotomy of consciousness by explaining passions in terms of physiology. It is also one of the dominant themes in works of fiction, whose numerous analyses might well serve as illustrations of the commonly accepted thesis.

Human reality appears then as a free power besieged by an ensemble of determined processes, and a strange gradation is set up. "One will distinguish wholly free acts, determined processes over which the free will has power, and processes which on principle escape the human-will."[3]

But how can we accept such a duality at the heart of the psychic unity? "How in fact could we conceive of a being which could be *one* and which nevertheless on the one hand would be constituted as a series of facts determined by one another—hence existents in exteriority—and which on the other hand would be constituted as a spontaneity determining itself to be and dependent only upon itself?"[4] How could such a spontaneity be capable of action on an already constituted mechanism of an entirely different nature from itself? How could will act upon passions in order to master them in accordance with the teachings of an age-old wisdom?

There are many such questions which remain unanswered. We do not understand. It is impossible to admit that consciousness is both free and determined; we must choose. Only two solutions are possible: either man is wholly free or he is wholly determined. Now, since he is not wholly determined—as philosophers will tell us—we must conclude that he is entirely free. Free in his emotions and in his passions, free in his voluntary acts. An example will illustrate our reasoning.

In the face of danger, we can adopt either of two attitudes: to face up to it or to yield to emotion. I may scream, tremble, flee, or even faint. I can also turn to face the danger and stand firm at all cost. In one case we speak of will power and courage, in the other of emotion and fear. And this is correct as far as it goes. This is how men fall into categories in difficult situations. Some are brave, others are cowards. But the mistake would be to praise the one and excuse the other. Military discipline rejects this attitude and it is right in so doing. One cannot speak of a freedom of courage and a determinism of fear. Freedom is there in all cases. Faced with the enemy, I was free to act reasonably by taking the usual steps toward self-defense. But I was also free to yield to the incoherent gestures of emotion. My choice alone was the decisive factor.

This is what Sartre thinks on the subject, and we are not surprised since we already know his views on emotion.

In fear, fainting and cataplexie aim at suppressing the danger by suppressing the consciousness of the danger. There is an *intention* of losing consciousness in order to do away with the formidable world in which consciousness is engaged and which comes into being through consciousness. Therefore we have to do with magical behavior provoking the symbolic satisfactions of our desires and revealing by the same stroke a magical stratum of the world.

The "voluntary and rational conduct" of the brave man, on the contrary,

will consider the situation scientifically, will reject the magical, and will apply itself to realizing determined series and instrumental complexes which will enable him to resolve the problems. It will organize a system of means by taking its stand on instrumental determinism.[5]

Thus, when faced with danger, the brave man and the coward both made a choice; one chose the magical aspect of the world, the other its technical aspect. And their choice was creative, so to speak. And it is we, with our freedom, who make it such.

But in this case the choice concerns only the means—the means for reaching a common end, which is to escape danger. Now this end itself might have been different. In a tricky situation, several interpretations are always possible. One might fight things, one might also adopt an attitude of indifference or of surrender. Here again we must choose. Freedom therefore governs the end as well as the means. One might say that it permeates all our activity.

Free to choose our conduct, we are also free to choose the causes which determine it—even when we think this is not the case; even when, in the voluntary act, we have deliberated carefully and at length over our motives. We have weighed the pros and cons; we were persuaded that we obeyed the strongest motives. And we are not wrong to think this. The partisans of a freedom of determination were right up to this point. But this very weight of the motive which settled the question originated in a choice we made. We know the phrase: when I deliberate, the chips are down. This amounts to saying that choice decided of the motives and not motives of the choice. Here again an example would be useful. The matter is of too much importance to allow the slightest misunderstanding.

What is apparently more deliberate than the escape of a prisoner? He must weigh his chances, evaluate the risks, decide if it is worth it. This is certainly a case where caution requires that one weigh the pros and cons with the greatest care. And yet, listen to what Mendès-France writes in the account of his activity:

> All the prisoners dreamt of escape during every single night of their confinement.
>
> For some it is a beautiful, vague and distant project which they know they would never try to carry out. For others it is an unforeseen eventuality, an occasion for which they are waiting without going out of their way to bring it about. For others again, it is a set decision, an appointment with adventure, with its vistas of freedom and its dangers.
>
> I do not believe there is such a thing as a chance escape. A prisoner who finds himself one day in an unforeseen situation, containing a possibility of escape,

will avail of it only if he has already chosen once for all, in his deepest being, to reclaim his freedom. An escape can sometimes be materially improvised, it is never improvised psychologically.[6]

This testimony was certainly not meant to illustrate a philosophical thesis. But as it stands, it is of the greatest interest. And it is unquestionably true: those who have been prisoners of war know very well that it is always the same ones, after several unsuccessful attempts, who finally get through the barbed wires, in spite of repeated threats, punishment, and maltreatment, and in spite of the danger. And it is not that they were more unhappy or had better opportunities for escape than the others, but simply because their preference went to freedom and they had chosen it.

They were like those workers who, in a period of revolution, rise up against the established order. In spite of what one might expect, those who revolt are not those who live most miserably, whose suffering is (so to speak) integrated in their being. In order to be able to react, one must first conceive of a new situation in which the endured miseries no longer exist. Then and only then will suffering become intolerable—when the project has been formed of no longer enduring it. "It is on the day that we can conceive of a different state of affairs that a new light falls on our troubles and our suffering and that we *decide* that these are unbearable."[7] Without this light, there is no will to change. Remember the people of Argos. Bearing the guilt for a crime they had not committed, they were the victims of a dreadful torment. Vengeful flies swarmed about them as on decaying flesh. And yet they did not protest; they endured, they accepted. They even refused the freedom Orestes brought to them. It was possible for them to cast off the yoke, to free themselves from Jupiter's whims. They chose remorse and its dreadful consequences as others choose misery and injustice. We see thus that freedom controls both the means and the ends of our actions.

Freedom Creates Values

And we immediately see what we must think of values. It is generally accepted that there are rules, imperatives, over which we have no control. They would be compelling and would govern our actions. There would be obligations and duties coming from without, whose origin should be sought in some authority. So that, in our search for an explanation, we would be referred back to society, science, or religion. But all this breaks down under closer scrutiny. Value is not a given, it is an ideal: freedom creates it and maintains or destroys it at will.

This is certainly what Mathieu is realizing in the striking revelation of *The Age of Reason:*

> The brake was suddenly slammed down and the bus stopped. . . . Mathieu thought: "No, it isn't heads or tails. Whatever happens, it is *by my agency* that everything must happen." Even if he let himself be carried off, in helplessness and in despair, even if he let himself be carried off like a sack of coal, he would have chosen his own damnation: he was free, free in every way, free to behave like a fool or a machine, free to accept, free to refuse, free to equivocate; to marry, to give up the game, to drag his dead weight about with him for years to come. He could do what he liked, no one had the right to advise him, there would be for him no Good nor

Evil unless he brought them into being. All around him things were gathered in a circle, expectant, impassive, and indicative of nothing. He was alone, enveloped in this monstrous silence, free and alone, without assistance and without excuse, condemned to decide without support from any quarter, condemned forever to be free.[8]

And we might also quote Orestes' famous apostrophe to Jupiter, in the same spirit and the same tones: "Suddenly, out of the blue, freedom crashed down on me and swept me off my feet. . . . And there was nothing left in heaven, no right or wrong, nor anyone to give me orders. . . . I shall not return under your law; I am doomed to have no other law but mine."[9]

Free for everything, free to accomplish, free to refuse, free to hesitate: we are thus in the presence of a freedom restricted by neither value nor reason.

But then, are we not once more faced with the dilemma we thought we had overcome? We began by saying it is not a question of unintelligibility nor of indeterminism, for we were convinced that freedom of indifference and submission to necessity were but forgeries of true freedom. And have we not stumbled against these obstacles once more? For if we escaped the claws of determinism, it is not clear that we have avoided caprice and arbitrariness. For what must we think of a freedom which determines motives and ends under all circumstances—whether important or not—and carries on thus as it pleases? Must we not speak of indifference and chance? We are reminded of Epicurus and Zeno once more. It is not easy to keep clear of philosophers!

Sartre, however, feels that the difficulty can be surmounted: to reject determinism is not to take refuge in

chance. Freedom of indifference and freedom of determination must both be rejected. The free act is not determined. There would be a contradiction in terms if we
claimed otherwise. But neither is it the gratuitous act of
which Gide speaks in *Les Caves du Vatican*. To be convinced of this, we need only turn to experience.

Suppose I go on a hike with some friends and I am
suddenly overcome with fatigue and obliged to sit down
on the side of the road. My weakness will certainly not go
unnoticed. It will be the object of unpleasant comments
rather than of pity. It is even likely that the hardiest of
my companions will reproach my lack of courage, of
tenacity, of will power, as though I were responsible for
my fatigue, as though I were free to yield to it or to
avoid it; in a word, as though my freedom were involved
in my weakness.

And yet, however strange it may seem, they are right.
They say I am responsible for my fatigue, and I am. It is
a behavior of defeat which lies within the control of my
freedom, just like any other behavior. Does this mean we
can speak of caprice? Certainly not. My fancy cannot control my attitude. I cannot start off again whenever I wish.
Fatigue is bearing down on me, paralyzing me. I must
endure it. I would like to get up and I cannot.

I cannot, this is true. However—and this is why I am
responsible—I could have. I could have, but at what price?
To alter this conduct with which I am so casually re-
proached, I would have had to undergo a complete change,
a genuine conversion. For we must go this deeply to find
the secret of victory or defeat, even in the simple matter
of a walk in the mountains.

But why does my tired friend persevere in his effort

when I collapse from weariness? It is because he loves his fatigue and "gives himself up to it as to a bath." It is his way of discovering the world and adapting to it.

> His fatigue is nothing but the passion he endures so that the dust of the highways, the burning of the sun, the roughness of the roads may exist to the fullest, his effort . . . is given as a way of appropriating the mountain, of suffering it to the end and being victor over it.[10]

He chose to master the mountain and in mastering it, to make it exist to the fullest, whereas I who threw down my knapsack and let myself fall down beside it, distrusted my body and the mountain. I wanted to get rid of my fatigue. I grasped it sternly, as something importunate incarnating "my body and my brute contingency in the midst of the world."[11]

Consciousness and Freedom Are One and the Same Thing

Thus the most commonplace behavior reveals an ensemble of projects without which it cannot be explained—an organic totality which represents the fundamental choice of myself. We must go as far as this essential freedom which gives their meaning to all my actions. This freedom is not a sort of "profound self" opposed, as Bergson thought, to a superficial self, but is rigorously simultaneous with all its manifestations. So a change in my actions implies a conversion of my being.

To be sure, such a conversion is possible. It is even possible every single instant.

One may recall the *instant* at which Gide's Philoctetes casts off his hate, his fundamental project, his reason for being, and his being. One may recall the *instant* when Raskolnikoff decides to give himself up. These extraordinary and marvelous instants when the prior project collapses into the past in the light of a new project which rises on its ruins and which as yet exists only in outline, in which humiliation, anguish, joy, hope are delicately blended, in which we let go in order to grasp and grasp in order to let go—these have often appeared to furnish the clearest and most moving image of our freedom. But they are only one among others of its many manifestations.[12]

In any case, as long as my fundamental choice does not change, my particular projects will not change either, or only within very narrow limits—even if I should want them to. My will, which is a *reflective attitude,* might influence my secondary projects, and in this sense it might "build me." But it will not in any way alter the initial project from which it originates itself. Besides, we can easily examine the role of the will and its limitations by means of some privileged experiences.

Psychoanalysis has familiarized us with the idea of inferiority complexes. And with good reason. One then chooses oneself "as inferior in the midst of others." Stuttering—with the annoyance and embarrassment it entails —can be a manifestation of this complex. We also know that stuttering can be cured. There are technical methods for this which can be quite effective with the cooperation of the will. Does this mean that the inferiority complex has been eradicated? Not at all. The infirmity has only been displaced. The will can act upon the stuttering, but not upon the complex. To modify the latter is to change the initial project; it is to perform a real conversion.

We do not see how one can talk of freedom of indifference under such circumstances, since everything in us depends upon a choice which might reveal itself to an existential analysis. But if we go no further, are we not leaving the question open? For if it is true that our particular acts are not indetermined, how about the fundamental choice which determines everything?

In other words, why this inferiority complex which is manifested by stuttering? Why this choice of myself-in-the-world which leaves me exhausted by the side of the road, while my companions, who are also tired, boldly go ahead? Why, among so many prisoners, do some escape while the others become resigned? Why, in *The Flies,* the choice of Orestes and of his sister Electra? Why again, these sensational conversions which are so disconcerting?

Obviously, there can be no answer. And we must admit that the choice which governs our conduct, often with the greatest flexibility, is purely gratuitous and unjustifiable. We might even say that it is absurd, since it is without reason. But the word is meaningless here since it makes sense only in a rational world and since this world exists only to the extent that, in choosing ourselves, we have chosen it. Our fundamental choice is therefore absurd, but "in this sense—that the choice is that by which all foundations and all reasons come into being, that by which the very notion of the absurd receives a meaning. It is absurd as being beyond all reasons."[13]

(Existence Precedes Essence

We are therefore led to the unquestionable conclusion that not only man is free, but consciousness and freedom are one and the same thing. There is no such thing as a human nature, a human essence of which freedom would be an attribute. If, as Leibniz thinks, Adam had been created by God and thus, if his essence had been fixed once for all, he would not have been responsible for his sin. Since he did not choose himself, he would not really have chosen his act. His fate would have been settled before "things were set in motion," just as peas are predetermined to be what they are. This amounts to saying that for man—to use the well-known phrase—existence precedes essence. "Man exists first, encounters himself, arises in the world and defines himself later." We must even say that strictly speaking he alone exists, in the sense in which existentialists understand the word, since he alone makes himself.

"Liberty—I sought it far away; it was so near that I couldn't touch it, that I can't touch it; it is, in fact, myself. I am my own freedom."[14]

NOTES

1. Jean-Paul Sartre, *Being and Nothingness* (New York: Citadel Press, 1966), p. 412.
2. *Ibid.*, p. 412.
3. *Ibid.*, p. 417.
4. *Ibid.*, p. 417.
5. *Ibid.*, p. 421.
6. P. Mendès-France, *L'Aurore*, July 30, 1954, p. 4.
7. Sartre, *op. cit.*, p. 411.
8. Jean-Paul Sartre, *The Age of Reason* (New York: Knopf, 1948), pp. 319-320.
9. Jean-Paul Sartre, *The Flies* (New York: Knopf, 1947), p. 158.
10. Sartre, *Being and Nothingness*, p. 431.
11. *Ibid.*, p. 433.
12. *Ibid.*, pp. 451–452.
13. *Ibid.*, p. 455.
14. Jean-Paul Sartre, *The Reprieve* (New York: Knopf, 1947), p. 362.

(IV)

Facticity and Situation

M an is free, and freedom is not a property of his being; it *is* his very being. Total, boundless, like that which Descartes conferred upon God, it is "at the level of the determination of essence by existence."[1]

But to proclaim the infinity of freedom in this way may seem very daring indeed, for facts are there which demand our reflection.

Autonomy and the Condition of Man

It is unquestionably true that each one of us is tied up with the lot of his class, of his nation, of his family, that he cannot conquer his appetites and habits, and that it is impossible to change the conditions of his birth: "I am born a worker, a Frenchman, an hereditary syphilitic, or a tubercular." It would be easy to expound all the influences which weigh upon us and seem to make man what he is.

And there is even more: when we try to confront the adversity of things, to avoid the snares they set for us, we are compelled—with the hope of securing only the feeblest results—"to obey nature in order to command it." It is strange freedom indeed, which leaves us no other choice than to submit or to give up.

And yet, these considerations, however indisputable, never discouraged the partisans of freedom. Not even Descartes, for whom the will is infinite and who advised us to "try to conquer ourselves rather than fortune." This is why it is possible to say, at the outset, that the action of our various determinations, however strong it may be, does not infringe upon freedom and, on the contrary, that it serves it.

But in order that this should not appear a paradox, we must first avoid the confusion ordinarily made by common sense. If freedom is understood to mean that one is able "to obtain what one has wished," it is obvious that we are never free. "The history of a life, whatever it may be, is the history of a failure," says Sartre. But the freedom of which the philosopher speaks is not synonymous with power. It is an autonomy of choice, with however—and this is important—

> a commencement of realization, in order that it may be distinguished from the dream and the wish. Thus we shall not say that a prisoner is always free to go out of prison, which would be absurd, nor that he is always free to long for release, which would be an irrelevant truism, but that he is always free to try to escape (or get himself liberated); that is, that whatever his condition may be, he can project his escape and learn the value of his project by undertaking some action.[2]

Having clarified this point, it remains that true freedom, which we say constitutes man, is the freedom of choice, and we are speaking of this freedom alone when we speak of consciousness. This freedom, like the free dom of "being able," seems to have limitations. It did not decide the existence of its being; it is not its own foundation. This privilege would be refused to God himself if he existed.

Where would this rash assumption lead us? We would then be compelled to admit that prior to the free choice of freedom we have the possibility of being-free or of not-being-free; that is, that there would be a previous freedom which would choose to be free, which would need another prior freedom in order to choose it, and so on. This is the very same difficulty as was encountered by those who tried to reduce consciousness to knowledge: the hypothesis is inadmissible.

Besides, even if it were acceptable, it would be of no use. It would not account for human reality. If we had chosen ourselves, we would have done it for some end and existence would be justified. But we know that it is not. We must therefore acknowledge that freedom is a *fact:* "we choose, but we do not choose to be free." and once more we can say that we are condemned to be free, which amounts to saying that we are both facticity and contingency, since they are one and the same thing: "Freedom is not free not to exist or not to be free."[3]

But this facticity does not prevent freedom from being infinite—in spite of the obstacles it encounters.

Freedom and the Past

First of all, let us examine the past. This question is of such importance as to require careful scrutiny, for there is no consciousness without past. When Descartes said his famous "I think, therefore I am" he should rather have said, "I think, therefore I was," for as soon as we exist the past is already there. "This is time, time laid bare, coming slowly into existence, keeping us waiting, and when it does come making us sick because we realize it's been there for a long time."[4]

Now what is the past? We recall the old quarrel between Ribot and Bergson at the beginning of this century. It was a matter of philosophy but even more of science, the latter being expected to settle the question. The idea was to discover the mechanism of memory and to use this knowledge to determine the very nature of the mind. Materialism or spiritualism, this was truly the point at issue.

Ribot followed the Cartesian tradition, at least on the subject of memory. Using the results of experimental research, he thought he could imprison memories in cerebral impressions—the idea of engrams was not yet in vogue—but this was to lose what had to be understood. The past reduced to some physiological modifications is no longer the past. It no longer has a face, for these impressions can only be actual. They belong to the present, and so do the images they retain and make appear. It will never be possible to constitute the dimension "past" out of these images, however much we may try, even by invoking the "myness" or the "intimacy" which would characterize their appearance.

Bergson, on the other hand, restores being to the past. In his view, events do not cease to be. They continue to be, they remain in their place, they constitute us. It is they who form the weave of the real "self," the "profound self." But while they do exist, they have lost their efficacy, they no longer act. It is not clear which forces lead this "unconscious" to "weave itself into the woof of our present consciousness."

For Ribot, the past *is not;* for Bergson, it *is,* but devoid of all efficacy and forever cut away from the present. For Sartre, the truth lies in neither of these solutions. It is not a question of "annihilating the past or of preserving for it the existence of a household god," but of considering the temporal phenomenon in its totality. "*My* past is first of all *mine;* that is . . . it exists as the function of a certain being which I *am.* The past is not *nothing;* neither is it the present; but at its very source it is bound to a certain present and to a certain future, to both of which it belongs."[5] This is what we must try to understand.

First, as we have seen, there is no consciousness without a past—an irremediable past. It is impossible to change in any way the events which mark our existence: birth, First Holy Communion, entrance to the university. It is also impossible to modify the events which have become part of my history and form the ensemble of my life, with its hopes, pleasures, joys, and torments. It is all fixed, petrified in its being, in the strong sense of the word. It is opaque, solid, in-itself. And in a sense we can say that this in-itself is us, since the past is "the ever growing totality of the in-itself which we are." A day will come when we will be nothing else. Once I am dead, "I shall be no more than my past. It alone will define me. . . . Death reunites us with ourselves. Eternity has changed us into ourselves."[6]

Like all stories, our story will come to an end—like that of Garcin in *No Exit.* This man is a coward during his life, and death takes him by surprise. Now he can no longer do anything about it: his cowardice and himself are one and the same thing. In the hell in which Sartre has placed him, he must face Inez, Inez the lesbian and the lucid, who is his consciousness and his mirror. He leaves his body up there on earth, in the hands of his friends. They are free to do what they please with it. He knows this and says: "I've left my fate in their hands . . . they're passing judgment on my life withut troubling about me, and they're right, because I'm dead."[7]

But the balance is a heavy one. It is hard to bear, even in hell. Garcin refuses to accept that cowardice in his realm. He protests. He tries to break out of the circle in which he is imprisoned. "I died too soon. I wasn't allowed the time to—to do my deeds." But Inez lashes back at him: "One always dies too soon—or too late. And yet one's whole life is complete at that moment, with a line drawn neatly under it, ready for the summing up. You are—your life, and nothing else."[8]

Our life and nothing else: that seems reasonable when the final stroke has been drawn. But before, when we are still alive, is the past identified with our being? And would a living Garcin be wrong to refuse to be imprisoned in his cowardice? There can be no doubt about the answer. To identify consciousness with the past would be to deny this very consciousness.

We said that "the past is the ever growing totality of the in-itself which we are." But we must add that "so long as we are not dead, we are not this in-itself in the mode of identity. *We have to be it,*"[9] which amounts to saying that in a sense I *am* my past and in another I *am not* my past.

Our history lies behind us. We can neither abolish it nor modify it. It is unchangeable past, our *substance* if you wish. But the present must assume this past, and give it a meaning, a direction, and hence its manner of being which is hardly anything else than its being, and this by putting itself at a distance, so that "the past is the in-itself which I am, but I am this in-itself as *surpassed*."[10] For example:

> Who shall decide whether that mystic crisis in my fifteenth year 'was' a pure accident of puberty or, on the contrary, the first sign of a future conversion. I myself, according to whether I shall decide—at twenty years of age, at thirty years—to be converted. The project of conversion by a single stroke confers on an adolescent crisis the value of a premonition which I had not taken seriously. Who shall decide whether the period which I spent in prison after a theft was fruitful or deplorable? I—according to whether I give up stealing or become hardened. Who can decide the educational value of a trip, the sincerity of a profession of love, the purity of a past intention, etc.? It is I, always I, according to the ends by which I illuminate these past events.
>
> Thus all my past is there pressing, urgent, imperious, but its meaning and the orders which it gives me I choose by the very project of my end.[11]

I assume it, I cast it off, or I modify its meaning, even when it seems to be crushing me. But this engagement I solemnly undertook and whose binding terms are weighing upon me will retain its value only to the extent that I do not break it. It is not the engagement that binds me, in spite of what I may sometimes think; it is I who bind myself through it.

Even my birth depends on me to some extent. Of course, as is often said, "I did not choose to be born," to be born here or there, in this milieu, in this class, in this family. Excuse or complaint? In any case, even my birth is not a brute fact. Like everything else it has a meaning, that very meaning which I bestow upon it. I may be ashamed of my birth, or astonished, or pleased. I can even think of committing suicide and thus assume my life as bad. In a sense, though I did not ask to be born, I choose to be born.

This means that all my past, however immutable, is suspended to my choice. It is therefore suspended to the present—but by the same token, to the future. For consciousness is project. It is perpetual flight, a flight from being, a flight toward that which will be. This allows us to understand the famous phrase—so baffling at first—which affirms that we are what we are not. The for-itself is not the past it is, and is the future it is not. For if we examine our consciousness carefully, we only find future in it, not only in our projects, in our expectations, but in the slightest of our gestures. "There is in my consciousness no moment which is not defined by an internal relation to the future; when I write, when I smoke, when I drink, when I rest, the meaning of my conscious states is always at a distance, down there, outside."[12]

Thus, whichever way and from whatever angle we look at the past, we see that it does not infringe upon our autonomy of choice, as it is also unaffected by the circumstances in which life sets us and which constitute our situation.

Freedom and Situation

Situation is also often pressing. And in many cases, just like the past, it is the object of excuses or complaints, because we are not willing to accept our responsibility for it.

War provides us with a beautiful example of this. War exonerates us from everything: tortures are part of war, the bombing of civilians is part of war, and so is the black market. We find the same reasoning in all countries and on all sides. But war itself? We usually say that only a few people are responsible for it, generally people who do not have to fight in it. All the others merely endure it as one would the plague or cholera. They are but victims. One is born for war or for peace in the same way as one is the son of a worker or of a bourgeois. It is all a matter of luck. Nothing can be done about it: facts speak for themselves, or at least this is the popular conception. And yet, Jules Romain dared write: "In war there are no innocent victims." And is this not true?

When Léon Bourgeois, in his attempt to justify his morality of solidarity, claimed that men are bound to society by a quasi-contract, he meant that by accepting to live in the same social group, we accept our share of duties and advantages, and that each one of us, depending on his situation, should consider himself both the debtor and the creditor of the whole group, solidarity being complete.

Now it is the very same with war. To be sure, no one will say we declared it (that is up to the politicians), or even that we wanted it (since we are the victims). But that is not really the point. Everybody has his own share of responsibility. Ours is as follows:

War has been declared and men are being mobilized. A choice must be made, my choice. Will I answer the call? Or will I refuse? Many will say that the question does not even arise since I am obliged to go, and yet the question *does* arise. For instead of allowing myself to be mobilized, whether because of spinelessness or cowardice or for some noble reason, I can choose to run the risk of deserting or even of committing suicide. In any case, as long as I take part in this war, in whatever capacity, it can be said that this war is my war because I chose it. The soldier is like the prisoner who is in a sense the accomplice of the warden if he does not keep on trying to escape.

It can even be said—and the paradox is only apparent —that the more difficult the circumstances, the more favorable they are to our freedom. It is then that we feel our abandonment and our dereliction most keenly and consequently also the need to make ourselves according to our own initiatives.

Sartre describes the Occupation in a manner which clearly illustrates this way of thinking.

> We were never more free than under the Nazi Occupation. We had lost all our rights, and first of all the right to speak. Every day we were insulted to our faces and could say nothing. Many of us were being deported, as workers, as political prisoners. . . . And yet, everywhere, on the walls, in the newspapers, on the screen, we saw this foul and insipid face which our oppressors wanted to tag onto us. Because of this we were free.[13]

We were all the more free that we could shift the responsibility of our initiatives and our choices onto no one. In those tragic circumstances, we were alone—alone and hunted. Alone in the face of arrests and insults. Alone before the almighty and self-confident oppressor. Alone to choose one's own condemnation by saying nothing or one's liberation by turning informer.

However much they may weigh upon us, circumstances do not restrict our freedom. And neither does the resistance of things when we confront them. We may think we are faced with an unsurmountable obstacle, but are we? Just look at that rock hanging over the road in front of me. To be sure, it belongs to the in-itself, and in this sense it is what it is and our freedom can do nothing about it. But I am not interested in it as such. It has no meaning for me. If it takes on a meaning, it is because my consciousness is there to give it. Will it lend itself to scaling or not? This does not concern the rock, it only concerns me. It becomes dangerous or manageable only because I made the project of scaling it. I might just as well have walked by without seeing it, or I might simply have stopped to admire it as a tourist. It is I, in all cases, who transform it into a protection or a threat, I who wrest it from its indifference by my admiration, my fear or my fondness for mountain climbing. Here again, it is not the situation which determines us, but we who determine ourselves.

And this leads us to try and establish the precise role of the given and that of the for-itself in the freedom-situation dyad. There is a given of which it must be said does not *cause* freedom (since it can produce only the given) nor is it the *reason* of freedom (since all reason comes into the world through freedom). Neither is it the *necessary condition* of freedom since we are on the level of pure contingency. Neither is it an *indispensable matter* on which freedom must exercise itself, for this would be to suppose that freedom exists ready-made as an Aristotelian form or as a Stoic Pneuma and that it looks for a matter to work in. The given in no way enters into the constitution of freedom since freedom is interiorized as the internal negation of the given. It is simply the pure contingency which freedom exerts by denying the given while making itself a choice; the given is the plenitude of being which freedom colors with insufficiency and with *négatité* by illuminating it with the light of an end which does not exist. The given is *freedom itself* in so far as freedom *exists*.[14]

Freedom and the World

And thus, by denying the in-itself, freedom discovers the world. In a frequently quoted passage, Simone de Beauvoir describes this unveiling. Françoise, the main character in *L'Invitée,* is walking through the theater where she works. Night has fallen. A smell of dust is rising from the dark halls. And in spite of the darkness, the red rug is faintly glowing. Then, one floor below, she sees the empty auditorium, the walls with their fresh coat of paint, the red plush chairs, the stage hidden behind its iron curtain: all this was waiting before she got there. "She would have liked to find the meaning of these deserted halls, of these sleeping objects; she was there and they belonged to her. The world belonged to her."[15]

The world, yes, but not the whole world. For that, "she would have had to be elsewhere, she would have had to be everywhere at once." But our condition does not allow for such an all-encompassing flight.

It is true that human reality is presence to the given, to the entire given, which means that it is a withdrawal from being, that it is its negation. We already know this. But if the for-itself went no further, if it were the negation of the totality of being, it would simply be nothingness. And this cannot be, since nothingness is not.

It is therefore clear that we are present to the world. But it is no less clear that at any given time we can only be present to this or to that. For it is beyond doubt that the world reveals itself concretely only "as the ground of each individual perception." Thus "the 'this' is the being which I at present *am not,* insofar as it appears on the ground of the totality of being. *This* is what I at present am not inasmuch as I have to be nothing of being."[16]

This can also be said in less technical language. Simone de Beauvoir writes that consciousness "can surpass the world only by becoming involved in it, that is, by condemning itself to apprehend in it a univocal and finite perspective, and thus to be infinitely and hopelessly overcome by it. It is necessary that I *lose* myself in the world for the world to exist."[17]

To lose oneself in the world in order that the world exist amounts to saying that "the world is human"; but not in the sense of the idealist, for whom the thing, which is realized beforehand, would be absolutely transparent. No, things are not to be contemplated; they are instruments, tools—they are exigencies. "Thus the world is revealed as haunted by absences . . . which point to it and determine it." It is a sort of mirror which, through our gestures and our acts, reflects our projects and our choices. In other words, it is a world of tasks.[18] And what had first appeared as an unsurmountable obstacle now comes to confirm our earlier claim.

We had said that man is free, that this freedom and his consciousness are one and the same thing, condemned that he is to make himself forever. We now know that the for-itself can exist and make itself only in relation to the in-itself. The past and our situation are therefore not obstacles. Facticity and contingency do not restrict transcendency.

"Past is the in-itself that I am" but "as surpassed." It does not coincide with me, at least not as long as I live. For it to be mine, I must be it, I must assume it. As for situation, it is my freedom that gives it its meaning and constitutes it, so that it is impossible to separate in the world that which belongs to the given from that which belongs to consciousness. The world is the "totality" which I am not. And the object, the "this," is the being which I am not at present as it appears on the ground of the totality of being.

We had also said that we are responsible and not only for our voluntary acts but for our emotions and our passions, for all our activity. We are therefore responsible for our existence. We can add that, just like our freedom, our responsibility has no limits, that it extends to the world of which we carry the full weight, for in choosing ourselves we choose all that is around us.

But man, when filled thus with the consciousness of his freedom and his responsibility, cannot help being seized with anguish, as we shall now see.

NOTES

1. Jean-Paul Sartre, *Being and Nothingness* (New York: Citadel Press, 1966), p. 445.
2. *Ibid.*, pp. 459–460.
3. *Ibid.*, p. 462.
4. Jean-Paul Sartre, *Nausea* (New York: New Directions Publishing, 1964), p. 46.
5. Sartre, *Being and Nothingness*, p. 86.
6. *Ibid.*, p. 91.
7. Jean-Paul Sartre, *No Exit* (New York: Knopf, 1947), p. 52.
8. *Ibid.*, p. 58.
9. Sartre, *Being and Nothingness*, p. 91.
10. *Ibid.*, p. 94.
11. *Ibid.*, p. 474.
12. *Ibid.*, p. 101.
13. Jean-Paul Sartre, *La République du Silence. L'Eternelle Revue*, I.
14. Sartre, *Being and Nothingness*, pp. 462–463.
15. Simone de Beauvoir, *L'Invitée* (Paris: Gallimard, 1943), p. 10.
16. Sartre, *Being and Nothingness*, p. 158.
17. Simone de Beauvoir, *Privilèges* (Paris: Gallimard, 1955), p. 207.
18. Sartre, *Being and Nothingness*, p. 175.

(V)

The Consciousness of Freedom: Anguish

Man felt nauseous when brought face to face with Being and its contingency. When faced with himself, he is seized with anguish. Anguish in the face of freedom, said Kierkegaard; anguish in the face of nothingness, replied Heidegger. In Sartre's view these two statements mean the same thing.

What then is this feeling which often inspired the lyricism of the prophets and whose echoes vibrate through the words of Pascal? It is important to find out, since it is another way of reaching the human reality which we are.

Anguish Is Not the Same Thing as Fear

Those who are accustomed to descriptions of our affectivity will immediately say that anguish is but a form of fear. At the very most they see a difference of degree. And language, by its very lack of precision, encourages this regrettable confusion. But in reality, there is a difference of nature between these two feelings, which can be best understood by comparing them.

It may well happen that a situation gives rise to both. Thus, the soldier who must endure the noise and perils of a bombardment will readily go from one to the other. Similarly, we speak both of fear and of anguish in connection with the man who is about to assume great responsibilities. But we must be sure to realize that they are not the same thing. "Fear," Sartre tells us, "is fear of beings in the world . . . whereas anguish is anguish before myself."[1] In other words, in fear the danger is without, outside me; in anguish it is within and grips me like vertigo.

We have all experienced this. It might have begun with fear. I am walking along a precipice. The path is narrow, without a guardrail. There is unquestionably the risk that I might slip on a stone or that the earth give way and I would inevitably fall into the abyss. I pay attention to where I set my foot, to rolling stones, to the slippery ground. I keep away from the edge of the path.

And then suddenly, when I think I am able to overcome the obstacle, everything is put in question anew, in a much more dangerous fashion. It is no longer the stone, the ground, the drop that I dread, but myself. Might I not throw myself over into this precipice which both horrifies and attracts me? So far I have progressed with caution, taking care not to fall. But I can no longer do it. I realize that it all depends on me, and I cannot depend upon myself. The danger is no longer exterior, it is within me.

In this physical situation, I am like the gambler who had resolved never to succumb to his passion again, and who finds himself, by chance, near the gaming table. It is true that the circumstances are completely different, but the same feeling is experienced. Vertigo or anguish—the ordeal is the same.

The gambler believed himself safe. He had decided not to gamble any more. But the table is there before him and all his self-confidence suddenly crumbles; he no longer knows what is going to happen. It is not that his resolution has changed in any way, or that it is even put in question again. He does not question whether he is right or wrong to turn away from the table. No, there is no inner debate; his decision still holds.

But he who did not want to risk financial ruin, he who did not want to disappoint his relatives, now feels that whereas his resolution has not changed, it has lost all its efficacy. The discouraging fact is there before him: the past does not control the future. The decision of yesterday remains valid only if I can recreate it today, if I recreate it constantly. But will it be recreated thus? And what guarantee have I that it will be? None whatsoever.

> *I must rediscover* the fear of financial ruin or of disappointing my family, etc., I must recreate it as experienced fear. It stands behind me like a boneless phantom. It depends on me alone to lend it flesh. I am alone and naked before temptation as I was the day before. After having patiently built up barriers and walls, after enclosing myself in the magic circle of a resolution, I perceive with anguish that *nothing* prevents me from gambling.[2]

And this is anguish indeed, this feeling which grips us when we realize that we are alone and helpless, separated from ourselves—from our past which has no other reality, no other efficacy than that we bestow upon it, but separated also from our future in which lay our projects and of which we cannot foretell, alone in the face of a world of possibilities which are our possibilities and which nothing compels us to realize.

Not even the oaths we take? Alain said that "our character is our oath." But even if this were so, we must not forget that an oath is valid and is held only because of me who takes it. It is as fragile as all my decisions, as uncertain as all my choices, for the Me of tomorrow is not announced by the Me of today. It remains a mystery, together with its promises and its disillusions. It is condemned to make itself in anguish.

Anguish is therefore inscribed in the condition of man, and it cannot be otherwise, since it is but the sense of our freedom, our self-consciousness. It is this truth which is bursting out in the famous dialog between Orestes and Jupiter, in *The Flies.*

> *Jupiter:* Your eyes are big with anguish, your face is pale and drawn. The disease you are suffering from is inhuman, foreign to my nature, foreign to yourself. Come back. I am forgetfulness, I am peace.
> *Orestes:* Foreign to myself—I know it. Outside nature, against nature, without excuse, beyond remedy, except what remedy I find within myself. But I shall not return under your law. I am doomed to have no other law but mine. . . . For I, Jupiter, am a man, and every man must find out his own way. Nature abhors man, and you too, god of gods, abhor mankind.
> *Jupiter:* That is true; men like you I hold in abhorrence.
> *Orestes:* Those words were a confession of your weakness. . . . You are God and I am free; each of us is alone, and our anguish is akin. . . . The folk of Argos are my folk. I must open their eyes.
> *Jupiter:* Poor people! Your gift to them will be a sad one; of loneliness and shame. You will tear from their

eyes the veils I had laid on them, and they will see their lives as they are, foul and futile, a barren boon.

Orestes: Why, since it is their lot, should I deny them the despair I have in me?

Jupiter: What will they make of it?

Orestes: What they choose. They are free; and human life begins on the far side of despair.[3]

Anguish Presupposes Reflection

Now if it is so, if man is freedom and if anguish is his lot, this is indeed a "permanent structure" of the human being; but then, how can we escape it so easily? For there are not only the people of the Coteau Vert, whom Antoine Roquentin sees coming and going every Sunday in the streets of Bouville, busying themselves with trifles, with smalltown pettiness, and with their mind at rest. They are not the only ones who seem to live a carefree existence, free from all anguish—there are all the others, and we too, all along the drab routine of daily life. The world in which we are immersed appears to be so well regulated that we do not at first see how anguish could possibly fit into it.

No sooner do I awaken in the morning than I become part of a mechanism which will release me only at night, when I go to sleep. My desk will draw me, with its books, the empty pages and the pencil beside them. And also my packet of tobacco. I roll my first cigarette and the machine is set in motion. I will write until other duties call me, a visitor to welcome, some business to transact. There will also be my meal, and the walk that follows it, during which I will meet my neighbor whom I will greet and with whom I will exchange a few trivialities—for such is the custom.

Everywhere thus, the road is already laid out, exigencies and urgencies are leading us. Just as the hunter rouses game, so our acts rouse values, all sorts of values: social, moral, political, and religious. Numerous are the books of laws and the catechisms which subject man to obligations and provide him with guardrails. (We need only think of those signboards covered with interdictions which so baffle the tourist visiting the German forests.)

Under such conditions, how can we still speak of anguish? And it is true that as long as we remain on the level of immediate action we will be spared this feeling. We are then in the realm of the spirit of seriousness, which demands that values be apprehended in terms of the social exigencies of the world. Like the people of Argos, veils are protecting us; we go about our business without asking questions, or at least no essential questions.

In order that anguish arise, it is necessary that this spirit, which is a spirit of laziness, should disappear. Reflection is necessary, for only then will the veil fall off and fullness give way to emptiness, so that we find ourselves faced with the real world, the world of freedom.

Let us examine ourselves. To be sure, there are inoffensive questions which lie within the realm of the spirit of seriousness. It is of little importance, for instance, that I ask the following questions concerning the book I am writing: Am I right to write this book—is it not a waste of time and effort, time which could be better spent? And besides, will I find a publisher willing to print it? There are many such questions, all on the level of immediate action.

But sometimes, interrogation reaches farther and deeper, to my true relation to the book. And this is how things happen. I have been "wanting to write this book," I took a keen interest in conceiving it, in outlining it. The first few chapters were a lot of work to be sure, but I enjoyed getting them organized. In any case, it is I who decided to write this essay, so that I cannot really understand myself now without taking into account this possibility which was one of my essential possibilities and which is now part of my essence, of my substance.

But I know that essence can only be in the past for me, and that the past does not control the present. It is not because I have been wanting, that I will go on wanting. I experience this every day. There is no constraint which I cannot escape. This desk which drew me to it yesterday, is repelling me today. Will I persevere in my work? I cannot be sure. For if I know that the past does not bind me, I also know that neither does my project. It has value only to the extent that I sustain it. My choice may decide, but it is I who decide of my choice. I am in front of the book to be written as the gambler in front of the gaming table —with a resolution that must be kept.

When I was content to act, to go ahead without thinking, the alarm clock rang. I got up, I washed, sat down at my desk, and all was well. The signboards were in their proper place and values were beckoning. There was no real problem; I stood on solid ground. But suddenly reflection came along, undermining and upsetting everything, for it is not simply a matter of the book I am writing but of every single one of my acts, however insignificant. I suddenly discover that I am the one who gives its meaning to the alarm clock, who, "by a signboard," forbid me to walk on the lawn, who decide of the interest of the pages

I am writing, who create those values which the world is constantly throwing back at me in the form of more or less pressing exigencies. I and no one else, so that

> I emerge alone and in anguish confronting the unique and original project which constitutes my being; all the barriers, all the guardrails collapse, nihilated by the consciousness of my freedom. I do not have nor can I have recourse to any value against the fact that it is I who sustain values in being. Nothing can ensure me against myself, cut off from the world and from my essence by this nothingness which I *am*. I have to realize the meaning of the world and of my essence; I make my decision concerning them—without justification and without excuse.[4]

Thus it is through anguish that I become conscious of my freedom, but anguish is a feeling that is hard to bear and it is difficult to become reconciled with it. Man loathes it as he does vertigo, so that the reflection which led us to it might run against conduct which brings us back to the facile appeasements of immediate action and of the spirit of seriousness.

> In each instance of reflection anguish is born as a structure of the reflective consciousness insofar as the latter considers consciousness as an object of reflection; but it still remains possible for me to maintain various types of conduct with respect to my own anguish—in particular, patterns of flight. Everything takes place, in fact, as if our essential and immediate behavior with respect to anguish is flight.[5]

We know for instance that Electra, after dreaming of the crime that would satisfy her thirst for vengeance and ensure her freedom, suddenly draws back from her brother when the dream becomes reality. Like the people of Argos, she refuses the liberating act and seeks refuge in remorse. To this unbearable anguish she prefers servitude, to freedom she prefers submission. She refuses to accept her responsibility.

And we do the same when an act appears too weighty and we ascribe it to some exterior force. "I didn't mean it," says the child in search of an excuse. And man often does the very same thing. But he finds excuses which the child would never think of. He accuses his nature, his character, and that which must explain both of them: heredity.

It is true that he has been encouraged to do this. Electra appealed to God. Today men are more sophisticated and only too eager to have recourse to the arguments of philosophers. Freedom is a nuisance, so we just declare that it does not exist. This is what the partisans of determinism are doing when they view belief in freedom as an illusion due to ignorance. It is because we do not know the cause of our acts that we think we are free. Bayle, a determinist through and through, illustrated his views by a familiar image: If the weathercock were conscious of its motion, it would not try to explain it by the too-subtle impulse of the wind whose action it would not feel, but would seek its origin within itself, in its own will. The same would be true of man, who is not an empire within an empire, as the saying goes. In reality, and whatever we may think, we belong to nature, we are subjected to its laws without ever being able to escape their rigorous consequences. The past determines the present, the present determines the future, and consciousness is but an endless succession of causes. We must therefore not speak of possibles which would be our possibles, but of a solid reality

with well-determined articulations, of a nature which produces our acts. We are thus reduced "to never being anything but what we are." Determinism "reintroduces in us
the absolute positivity of being-in-itself and thereby rein-
states us at the heart of being."[6]

But unfortunately, determinism is but a theory of philosophers and scientists. It is but an hypothesis, a postulate.
It avails nothing against the evidence of my freedom and
the ensuing sense of anguish. One cannot disarm a feeling
with ideas. What is the use of telling a child that his fears
and pains are useless, or telling a man experiencing a hal-
lucination that he is being misled? Determinism, therefore, can abolish anguish only to the extent that it is a
belief rather than an idea. Anguish placed under judgment is not a disarmed anguish. A more concrete effort of
flight is necessary, which must operate on the level of
reflection. And it is this effort which is expressed in a
double attempt at distraction.

Attempts At Distraction

Distraction is, first of all, "in relation to the possible
opposed to *my* possible." It is obvious that I can write this
book, or I can not write it. But I try to apprehend this
latter eventuality "as needing to be mentioned merely as
a reminder, as not concerning me." It would not be a living project which could become my project and would
thus be a threat for me, but rather a purely conceivable
hypothesis, devoid of all efficacy. In other words, it is an
eventuality which might be that of another, so that the
chosen possible (in this case the book I am writing) "would
appear—due to this selection—as my only concrete possible."[7] Sartre continues:

But flight before anguish is not only an effort at distraction before the future; it attempts also to disarm the past of its threat. What I attempt to flee here is my very transcendence insofar as it sustains and surpasses my essence.[8]

Bergson provides us with the best expression of this effort; we all know this flexible and subtle analysis of "the immediate givens of consciousness," his criticisms of determinism and of free choice, and also his distinction between the profound self and the superficial self, which provides him with a solution to the problem of freedom. For Bergson, there is a

profound self which endures and organizes itself, which is constantly contemporary with the consciousness which I have of it and which cannot be surpassed by consciousness, which is found at the origin of my acts not as a cataclysmic power but as a father begets his children, in such a way that the act without following from the essence as a strict consequence, without even being foreseeable, enters into a reassuring relation with it, a family resemblance. The act goes farther than the self but along the same road; it preserves, to be sure, a certain irreducibility, but we recognize ourselves in it, and we find ourselves in it as a father can recognize himself and find himself in the son who continues his work.[9]

This is just another way of fleeing from anguish by trying to disarm the past, but these attempts are of no avail. If they were, they would only result in the destruction of consciousness. For all these efforts at distraction consist in trying "to apprehend ourselves from without as an Other," and thus reducing ourselves to the status of a thing, which is impossible. We cannot—to use Sartre's terminology—prevent those possibilities which contradict our possibilities from being living possibilities, nor—as Bergson would have it—conceive our freedom as a metaphysical property "driven down into the heart of an opaque being." In reality, anguish is the true "immediate given" of our freedom.

It is therefore impossible to stifle or even to really hide it. It is not an external object from which we can turn our look or our attention.

> If I *am* what I wish to veil, the question takes on quite another aspect. I can in fact wish 'not to see' a certain aspect of my being only if I am acquainted with the aspect which I do not wish to see. This means that in my being I must indicate this aspect in order to be able to turn myself away from it; better yet, I must think of it constantly in order to take care not to think of it.[10]

To deny anguish is therefore always a mode of being conscious of it. But we are then dealing with "a particular type of conduct." We are dealing with *bad faith*.

NOTES

1. Jean-Paul Sartre, *Being and Nothingness* (New York: Citadel Press, 1966), p. 29.
2. *Ibid.*, p. 33.
3. Jean-Paul Sartre, *The Flies* (New York: Knopf, 1947), pp. 158–160.
4. Sartre, *Being and Nothingness*, p. 39.
5. *Ibid.*, p. 40.
6. *Ibid.*, p. 40.
7. *Ibid.*, p. 42.
8. *Ibid.*, p. 42.
9. *Ibid.*, p. 42.
10. *Ibid.*, p. 43.

(VI)

The Refusal of Anguish:
Bad Faith

We know that anguish is "a permanent structure of the human being." And we can already add that bad faith is another. The whole of Sartre's work bears witness to this.[1]

Bad Faith Is Common to All Men

When Antoine Roquentin visited the museum of Bouville, it was neither with the appropriate admiration of the man in the street nor with the artist's concern for aesthetics. He was not so interested in the paintings themselves as in what they represented; through the portrait he reached for the man, judging him without mercy.

Apart from the bachelor "naked to the waist, his body a little green, like that of a dead man," and who "by a harsh and well-deserved punishment" had no one by his deathbed to close his eyes, there were all the others, the past dignitaries of the town, more than a hundred and fifty of them, whose portraits presented their proud faces to their best advantage.

With the exception of a few young people, prematurely taken from their families, and the Mother Superior of a boarding school, none of those painted had died a bachelor, none of them had died childless or intestate, none without the last rites. Their souls at peace that day as on other days, with God and the world, these men had slipped quietly into death, to claim their share of eternal life to which they had right. For they had rights to everything: to life, to work, to wealth, to command, to respect, and finally, to immortality.[2]

At peace with God and with men, on their dying day as they had been throughout their life, what had these leaders really been like? Pharisees who, without the slightest illusions, acted a part. And it is indeed quite true that there was a great deal of conformity and hypocrisy in these self-satisfied men whose portraits so irritated Roquentin. But were they exceptional in any way? It would seem not. Their faces, with their sharp features, look like many other faces. And their stilted attitude is but an exaggerated version of the attitude of most people. "Swine" [*salauds*] said Roquentin, but they were no more swine than all those who seek refuge in reassuring myths, who believe in absolute values, in rights and duties inscribed in nature, those who find comfort in the "spirit of seriousness."

This comfort Lucien Fleurier will find in *L'Enfance d'un Chef*. What questions did this adolescent not ask? What solitary meditations, what efforts to try to become a man? He did all this until the day he adopted the liberating phrase: "I have rights." Rights are something like triangles and circles—so perfect they do not exist. One could draw thousands of round figures with the help of a pair of compasses without ever being able to realize a single circle. In the same way, generations of workers might obey Lucien's orders without ever exhausting his right to command. Rights are beyond existence, they are like mathematical objects or religious dogmas. He had thought for a long time that he existed by accident, completely adrift, but that was only because he had not thought enough. Long before he was born, his place had been set. Long before his father's marriage, he had been awaited; he had been born only to fill this place. I exist, he thought, because I have the right to exist. An hour earlier, a slender and hesitant adolescent had entered the café: it was a man who now walked out of it, "a leader among the French."[3]

He is a leader, in a sense, for that is what people will think of him. But one could equally well say "a swine." Lucien Fleurier has just sought shelter in easy appeasements. Like the leaders of Bouville, he fled from this anguish that was tormenting him; he refused to accept his responsibility.

But this refusal can sometimes take on a collective form and it then leads to the worst aberrations. Thus, anti-Semitism is common in European countries. One might have thought for a while that the downfall of Hitler had dealt a deadly blow to an ideology of which one had been able to measure the atrocious consequences. But insidious propaganda began steadily to increase: first unpleasant rumors spreading by word of mouth, then, in turn hypocritical and violent declarations. To be sure, one does not go so far as to sanction the atrocities of the concentration camps. In fact, any such intentions are adamantly disclaimed. But one is quite willing to condone measures which would prevent the Jew from doing any harm; for today as yesterday, he is felt to be responsibile for all our evils. "Through him Evil arrives on the earth. All that is bad in society (crises, wars, famines, upheavals, and revolts) is directly or indirectly imputable to him."

The anti-Semite, therefore, appears to be afraid of the Jew. But in fact, this is not at all the case. It is of himself and of the world that he is afraid. What he really dreads is to suddenly discover that the world is ill-contrived, that he must invent and modify, and must carry the burden of his "agonizing and infinite responsibility."

This is how Sartre presents him to us in his deplorable reality: a man afraid of himself,

> of his own consciousness, of his liberty, of his instincts, of his responsibilities, of solidariness, of change, of society, and of the world—of everything except the Jews. He is a coward who does not want to admit his cowardice to himself; a murderer who represses and censures his tendency to murder without being able to hold it back, yet who dares to kill only in effigy or protected by the anonymity of the mob; a malcontent who dares not revolt from fear of the consequences of his rebellion. . . . The existence of the Jew merely permits the anti-Semite to stifle his anxieties at their inception by persuading himself that his place in the world has been marked out in advance, that it awaits him, and that tradition gives him the right to occupy it. Anti-Semitism, in short, is fear of the human condition. The anti-Semite is a man who wishes to be pitiless stone, a furious torrent, a devastating thunderbolt—anything except a man.[4]

So if the Jew did not already exist, we would invent him. Americans, who do not have him—at least not in the same way as Europeans—have a substitute: the Negro, who symbolizes in their mind the evil of humanity. It is always this same desire to shift onto someone else the responsibility we are refusing, always the same projection and the same catharsis. But it is also always the same lie, for all these people are gratuitous and unjustifiable beings. If they were not, they would not be men. And when they flee their responsibilities, when they deny their freedom and their anguish, they are lying to themselves.

Bad Faith Is a Lie

But can we really speak of a lie in this case? How could consciousness deceive itself? Lying to another creates no problems since there is a deceiver and a deceived. A deceiver knows the truth and knows it completely, for if he were in ignorance or in error, if he were the dupe of his words, of his statements and of his insistence, he would not really be a liar. A deceived does not know and falls victim to an intention he does not suspect. Thus the lie is but a regrettable utilization of the duality of "myself" and "myself in the eyes of others." It is because my consciousness is hidden from the others that I can lie to them.

For bad faith, it is quite a different matter. We must speak of a lie since one is trying to hide a displeasing truth, or to present as truth a pleasing untruth. But now there is no distinction between the deceived and the deceiver. They are the same person. Bad faith does not come from outside; I do not endure it. It is I myself who affect myself with it. I must know the truth since I am lying and at the same time I must not know it since I am deceived. And this at the very same moment. If the first condition were not realized, I would be in good faith; if the second were lacking, we would be dealing with cynicism. In either case there would be no lie.

And yet consciousness is translucent. How then could it simultaneously know and not know? We are faced with quite a problem. On the one hand bad faith presents "an autonomous and durable form. It can even be the normal aspect of life for a very great number of people." On the other hand, we must admit that we find it difficult to understand this paradoxical attitude.

Will we resort to the concept of the unconscious to help us to solve this problem? Psychoanalysts invite us to do it. They say that if we only consider the information given by consciousness, we will often be mistaken as to the meaning of our conduct, and they explain why this is so.

It can happen, for instance, that on walking past a bookstall I feel the urge to steal a book. The impulse is irresistible, the action dishonest, I do not understand. Will I question myself and try to find excuses? I can find any amount of reasons: the book is rare, it is of great interest to me, it is too expensive for me to buy. But of what value are these arguments? As far as the psychoanalyst is concerned, they are of no interest. He knows that at the origin of my impulse there is a process derived from self-punishment which is attached more or less directly to an Oedipus complex. And introspection will never reveal this since complexes belong to the realm of the unconscious. Thus, in order to discover the true explanation, I need the cooperation of a professional psychoanalyst, unless I myself, with my knowledge of psychoanalysis, can judge myself from without, like a physician diagnosing his own ailment.

For we know, since Freud, that there are within us unconscious instincts, drives and complexes which remain active forces, but whose direct expression is blocked by an unconscious censorship. When these forces are revealed to consciousness, it is through fears, forgetting, or dreams

—that is, through a symbolization which one must know how to interpret in order to find its true meaning, or at least its most probable meaning, for we are here within the realm of scientific hypothesis.

> Thus psychoanalysis substitutes for the notion of bad faith, the idea of a lie without liar; it allows me to understand how it is possible for me to be lied to without lying to myself since it places me in the same relation to myself that the other has in respect to me; it replaces the duality of the deceiver and the deceived, the essential condition of the lie, by that of the 'id' and the 'ego.'[5]

We would thus be rid of an embarrassing concept, and all would be fine—if only the explanation held up under more careful scrutiny. Unfortunately, the psychoanalysts' theory collapses if we examine ourselves more closely.[6] They tell us of an unconscious censor who would be responsible for our repressions. But this repressive action is not performed at random—the censor must constantly choose between those drives which, by principle, should touch on consciousness. Some are entitled to be expressed, such as the essential needs—hunger and thirst for instance, as well as certain lawful sexual impulses. Others are condemned—these are usually of the sexual order. There is therefore a continual selection. But how can this be explained if the censor is unconscious?

Moreover, from another point of view, the action of the censor, as it is presented, remains shrouded in mystery. We know that psychoanalysis is combined with a therapeutic method. In fact that is how it started. Freud himself and all specialists after him, will admit that the patient sometimes resists and shuts himself off in an attitude of mistrust; he refuses to speak or gives fantastic accounts of his dreams. Sometimes he even discontinues the treatment. And here again, whence the resistance?

It does not come from the conscious "ego" which, by definition, does not know whether the psychiatrist is getting close to the cause of the ailment. Moreover, if the patient did know, he would not resist. He would help, since he wishes to get better. Neither does it emanate from the repressed complexes which, if left to their own devices, would collaborate effectively toward the success of the treatment, for they aim at expressing themselves and therefore try to elude and play tricks on the censor when they can do no more.

Under these conditions—and this is the only plausible hypothesis—it is up to consciousness to make a choice between our drives, and it is fully aware of so doing, since in order to choose, it must first be conscious (of) itself.

> How could the censor discern the impulses needing to be repressed without being conscious of discerning them? How can we conceive of a knowledge which is ignorant of itself? . . . Thus the resistance of the patient implies at the level of the censor an awareness of the thing repressed as such, a comprehension of the end toward which the questions of the psychoanalyst are leading, and an act of synthetic connection by which it compares the *truth* of the repressed complex to the psychoanalytic hypothesis which aims at it. These various operations in their turn imply that the censor is conscious (of) itself. But what type of self-consciousness can the censor have? It must be the consciousness (of) being conscious of the drive to be repressed, but precisely *in order not to be conscious of it.*[7]

This brings us back where we started. Since it is impossible to explain bad faith by means of a censor, the latter being itself an attitude of bad faith, we are still faced with the same difficulty: how is it possible that man can lie to himself?

Sartre's Explanation

In Sartre's view, the only way of settling the question is to examine two conducts which strike him as particularly significant.

First, he considers a woman who is going out with a particular man for the first time. "She knows very well the intentions which the man who is speaking to her cherishes regarding her," and that she will soon have to make a decision. But for the time being "she concerns herself only with what is respectful and discrete in the attitude of her companion." She would indeed be humiliated to be merely an object of desire, and yet she does not want a respect that would be only respect. "In order to satisfy her, there must be a feeling which is addressed wholly to her *personality*—that is, to her full freedom—and which would be a recognition of her freedom." But the man then takes her hand. Will she withdraw it? Certainly not! That would break the spell. But she leaves it there without noticing it.

> She *does not notice* because it happened by chance that she is at this moment all intellect. She draws her companion up to the most lofty regions of sentimental speculation; she speaks of life, of her life, she shows herself in her essential aspect—a personality, a consciousness. And during this time the divorce of the body from the soul is accomplished; the hand rests inert between the

warm hands of her companion— neither consenting nor resisting—a thing.[8]

We now turn to the attitude of the homosexual who refuses to accept the opinion people have of him. He does not want to be an object of scorn for all those around him. It is true that he has been a homosexual, but he is not one. He is not a homosexual in the manner of a thing, in the manner that a stone is a stone. He is free, that is, beyond all the definitions in which people are trying to confine him. And he is right to make these claims. Just as Garcin, in *No Exit,* would have been right to refuse his reputation of cowardice if precisely he had not been in hell. For as long as a man lives, he retains all his possibilities of acceptance and refusal. He can always escape and flee, leaving his tattered garments in the hands of those who are tracking him down. The pederast is therefore right to reject the view that his habits constitute for him a destiny—but his desire to remain out of reach will lead him beyond this legitimate refusal. They say he is a homosexual, but he will proclaim that he is not, absolutely and definitively. He uses the same language as his detractors, though in the opposite direction. And he makes the same mistake.

We have here two conducts of bad faith bringing us to the heart of the problem. Man is facticity and transcendence, and he is playing here on this dual aspect of human reality. He affirms their identity while preserving their differences "in such a way that in the instant when a person apprehends the one, he can find himself abruptly faced with the other."

In the case of the young woman, we see the affirmation of facticity as being transcendence. Words and gestures are disarmed of their true meaning, not with a view to eliminating the pleasure they give her, but on the contrary to raise it beyond physical desire. The woman

> has disarmed the actions of her companion by reducing them to being only what they are; that is, to existing in the mode of the in-itself. But she permits herself to enjoy his desire, to the extent that she will apprehend it as not being what it is, will recognize its transcendence. Finally while sensing profoundly the presence of her own body . . . she realizes herself as *not being* her own body and she contemplates it as though from above, as a passive object to which events *can happen,* but which can neither provoke them nor avoid them because all its possibilities are outside of it.[9]

For the homosexual, who "frequently has an intolerable feeling of guilt," we have the reverse process: transcendence is reduced to facticity. He asserts his freedom in order to escape from the in-itself. But in reality he does not escape from it; he merely leaves one facticity to seek refuge in another. The homosexual claims he is not a homosexual as though a table could become an inkwell. He refuses the judgment of the others in the name of freedom. But this freedom, now that it has served its purpose, he sees as a thing.[10]

Bad Faith, the Ontological Malady of Consciousness

And thus, in the light of this double description, we see that the possibility of bad faith is not such a problem as we had first thought. It is related to the ambiguity of our human condition, to this painful conflict within our consciousness which we all know so well. And it is the opposite, sincerity, which is impossible.

Of course, there is a way of being sincere which is

undeniable: that which consists of expressing exactly what happened. I confess that at a certain moment I felt pleasure, or sorrow, and I am telling the truth. But this is not sincerity as it is usually understood. Sincerity "aims at itself in present immanence" and would lead, if successful, to the perfect coincidence of self with self. When understood in this way, it is never a state but an ideal, an ideal that cannot be realized since it is impossible for consciousness, so long as it remains consciousness, to coincide with itself.

In reality, we are always in a situation analogous to that of the café waiter who is playing at being a café waiter. To be sure, he is a café waiter in the sense that he is neither a diplomat nor a reporter, but this is only a representation. His attitude, his gestures, his constant application are sufficient proof that he plays his part as an actor plays his. The same is true of the good speaker who plays at speaking because he cannot *be speaking,* or of the attentive pupil who, in his efforts to play his role, ends up by no longer hearing anything at all. "Perpetually absent to my body, to my acts, I am despite myself that 'divine absence' of which Valéry speaks."[11]

But are there not some attitudes which contradict these views? Thus, this deep overwhelming sorrow I feel after the loss of someone dear to me, would be odious if its sincerity were questioned. And yet, even there I am not what I think I am. I make myself sad, but I am not sad. "The being of sadness escapes me by and in the very act by which I affect myself with it."[12] Besides, if circumstances require it—in the presence of a visitor for instance—I temporarily cast off my sadness to take it up again later.

We must therefore agree that the ideal of sincerity is a task which cannot be filled and that the "normal" attitude of consciousness is bad faith. Not that this bad faith is strictly speaking deliberate, nor that it is the result of a "reflective, voluntary decision." But it is "a spontaneous determination of our being. One *puts oneself* in bad faith as one goes to sleep, and one is in bad faith as one dreams."[13] Thus we are dealing neither with the obvious nor with the cynical lie, which should not surprise us since faith of any kind is belief. And to believe, as we know, is always not to believe. "One never wholly believes what one believes," says Sartre.

It remains nonetheless that bad faith is an "immediate, permanent threat to every project of the human being." It is the refusal of our condition, of the freedom and the anguish which constitute us. The first act of bad faith is to flee what one cannot flee, to flee what one is. And it is this refusal, as we shall see, which constantly imperils our relations with the others.

NOTES

1. Cf. R.-M. Albérès, *Jean-Paul Sartre: Philosopher Without Faith*, trans. Wade Buskin (London: Merlin Press, 1964).
2. Jean-Paul Sartre, *Nausea* (New York: New Directions Publishing, 1964), pp. 113–114.
3. Jean-Paul Sartre, *Le Mur* (Paris: Gallimard, 1939).
4. Jean-Paul Sartre, *Anti-Semite and Jew* (New York: Schocken Books, 1948), pp. 53–54.
5. Jean-Paul Sartre, *Existential Psychoanalysis*, translation of several chapters of *L'Etre et le Néant* (New York: Philosophical Library, 1953), p. 215.
6. In her introduction to *La Transcendence de l'Ego* (nouvelle edition 1965, p. 8), Sylvie Le Con tells us that Sartre "has completely abandoned his past views, his refusal of the unconscious and of psychoanalytical understanding and would no longer uphold his past claims on the subject. . . ."
7. Sartre, *Existential Psychoanalysis*, pp. 218–219.
8. *Ibid.*, pp. 227–228.
9. *Ibid.*, pp. 228.
10. *Ibid.*, pp. 250–252.
11. *Ibid.*, p. 240.
12. *Ibid.*, p. 243.
13. *Ibid.*, p. 263.

(VII)

The Confrontation of Freedoms

Inseparable from Being, which is simultaneously repelling and fascinating him, at grips with himself in anguish and bad faith, man is condemned to make himself, but not in solitude. He makes himself in the presence of the Other. It is true that "I emerge alone in the face of the unique and primordial project which constitutes my being" and it is I who "decide alone—without justification or excuse" the meaning of the world of my essence; it is true that I must bear my existence and no one else can assume responsibility for it in any way; but these considerations, however weighty, should not lead us to the reef of solipsism. I make myself, that is true; but I make myself among the others. It would be sheer madness to say otherwise.

Philosophers Are Mistaken

Once again, philosophers are of little use. They affirm but do not prove. First, if we listen to the realists, we apprehend exterior reality, and among it, objects of a particular type—bodies, whose attitudes and gestures are signs which must be interpreted in the light of our own experience. Thus tears and laughter will convey the suffering and the joy of the Other, because in the same circumstances we have cried and laughed. And the same is true of language, an ensemble of movements and sounds, which is meaningful to the extent that we ourselves speak, which amounts to saying that

> my body as a thing in the world and the Other's body are the necessary intermediaries between the Other's consciousness and mine. The Other's soul is therefore separated from mine by all the distance which separates first my soul from my body, then my body from the Other's body, and finally the Other's body from his soul.[1]

The trip from my consciousness to that of the Other is therefore a long one. If only it could lead to the desired certainty! But an exacting mind cannot be satisfied with such an enterprise. As Bergson once told his audience at the University of Birmingham:

> If we seek for mathematical certainty, we shall obtain nothing, for you cannot even be mathematically sure that I, who am speaking to you at this moment, possess a consciousness. I might be a well-constructed automaton—going, coming, speaking—without internal consciousness, and the very words by which I declare at this moment that I am a conscious being might be words pronounced without consciousness.[2]

No doubt, he went on, this would be unlikely; it is the opposite that is probable, in view of the analogies existing between you and me—and the probability is such as to be practically equivalent to a certainty. But it remains that Bergson's practical equivalency does not absolutely justify the feeling we have of the Other's existence. Men or automata? There can be no definite answer, since there is no final proof.

Will idealism give us this proof? Indeed it will not. Here we do not leave the realm of representations where we established ourselves from the very beginning: the Other becomes the condition of our own experience of the world. We are in the presence of "organized forms such as gestures and expressions, acts and conducts," which refer us to an "organizing unity which on principle is located outside of our experience."[3] So the experience of the Other is simply a hypothesis which allows us to put some order and coherence in our thought; it does not open up onto certainty. And even if it did, it would be no use— the Other would only be for us an *object* of representation whereas he is *consciousness* and *subject*.

Realists and idealists therefore leave us faced with the same impossible choice: either to stick to the exigencies of a rigorous logic and shut ourselves up as madmen in the impregnable blockhouse of solipsism (to quote Schopenhauer) or, following our deepest inclinations, to make an act of faith in the plurality of consciousnesses. But in either case our attitude is unreasonable, and it cannot be otherwise. Once we accept the postulate that consciousness, at the outset, is closed in upon itself, how can we ever hope to wrench it from its solitude?

But this postulate of classical philosophy is false, and the problem it raises is pointless. As Hegel saw it—and after him Husserl and Heidegger—consciousness is not first of all closed in upon itself in such a way that it can only reach the Other through a reasoning with a more or less probable outcome. No, we must not search for the

Other outside us. He is in us, in our heart. He is a presence; a presence which Sartre says reveals itself to each one of us through a familiar conduct: shame. Just as nausea and anguish had brought us in the presence of freedom and of ourselves, respectively, so shame would place our consciousness before the Other. We are going to see how.

Suddenly I feel my face reddening, I find it difficult to control my speech and my movements, I hesitate, I stammer, my mouth feels dry.

> It is as though the impetus which bore me and with which I coincided, suddenly fell back upon me just as the mass of water in a wave comes to flatten out upon itself all the force that pushed it toward the shore. What has happened?[4]

It is true that the movement I just made was clumsy and awkward. I upset a table, a chair perhaps—but we must admit that it was of no great importance. At the very most it might have called for a movement of impatience or even a smile. And even in the event of a more serious indiscretion, such as peering through a keyhole or eavesdropping, why did this all-absorbing activity suddenly become a paralyzing attitude, *without the slightest reflection* on my part? Why this feeling which affects me so keenly? Because consciousness is always consciousness of something, whichever way you look at it. It has an object, and here the object is me. It is of myself I am ashamed. Once more, why? There can only be one answer: while I was acting, I felt—with good reason or not, it does not matter—that I was being seen. Alone I would not have experienced anything of the sort; but the Other was looking at me while I was being clumsy or indiscrete, and there lay the problem.

The Look and Its Consequences

The Other is the look, whatever way it may manifest itself. Usually it is through the eyes;

> but the look will be given just as well on occasion when there is a rustling of branches, or the sound of a footstep followed by silence, or the slight opening of a shutter, or a light movement of a curtain. During an attack men who are crawling through the brush apprehend as a *look to be avoided*, not two eyes, but a white farmhouse which is outlined against the sky at the top of a little hill. . . . Now the bush, the farmhouse are not the look; they only represent the *eye*, for the eye is not at first apprehended as a sensible organ of vision but as the support of the look. They never refer therefore to the actual eye of the watcher hidden behind the curtain, behind a window in the farmhouse. In themselves they are already eyes. On the other hand neither is the look one quality among others of the object which functions as an eye, nor is it the total form of that object, nor a 'worldly' relation which is established between that object and me. On the contrary, far from perceiving the look *on* the objects which manifest it, my apprehension of a look turned toward me appears on the ground of the destruction of the eyes which 'look at me.' If I apprehend the look, I cease to perceive the eyes.[5]

This is so true that when we apprehend the look, we no longer know the color of the eyes, nor whether they are beautiful or not. It is as though they were hidden from us. We are simply in the presence of the Other. And this is how we encounter the Other. I do not constitute him the Other; his existence is for me a "contingent and irreducible" fact, which means that between the Other and me there is not primarily a relation of knowledge to knowledge, but of being to being; it is in terms of my being that the problem of the Other arises.

And this problem arises in such a way as to involve very serious consequences. As long as I thought I was alone, everything was so easy: the world was my own. Objects were there on display, organized and classified. I was in my universe. In the public park, for instance, I saw the lawn, the bench, the trees. I could estimate distances. I mastered all meanings: tools or obstacles, all things were dependent upon my intentions. They were what I chose to make them. Even that human form over there, slumped down on a bench, is but an object among other objects.

But precisely, this form is not a statue. It is a man—an object, thus, since it is there a few yards away from me, but not an ordinary object. The body of the Other is significant, it exists "only in and through a transcendence," and as far as I am concerned its presence is a constant threat, and might make my universe disintegrate at any time. It is true that the man may be dreaming or sleeping and is thus not conscious of the garden around him, and the distintegration is then purely virtual. But he may also unfold his own distances around him and it then appears to me "that the world has a kind of drain hole in the middle of its being and that it is perpetually flowing off through this hole." Furthermore,

the appearance of the Other in the world corresponds therefore to a fixed sliding of the whole universe, to a decentralization of the world which undermines the centralization which I am simultaneously effecting. But

> *the Other* is still an object *for me*. He belongs to *my distances*.[6]

But now the man sits up and looks at me, and everything is completely changed. From now on, objects are no longer my objects, distances are no longer my distances and meanings are no longer my meanings; the universe is constantly escaping me. The Other is stealing the world from me.

What happens to me during this strange experience? We turn to Daniel in *The Reprieve:*

> It clove him like a scythe, amazing, awful, and delightful. . . . *They* see me—no, not even that: *it* sees me. He was *the object* of looking. A look that searched him to the depths, pierced him like a knife-thrust, and was not his own look.[7]

For the look of the Other does indeed pierce through us. And not to spur on my consciousness, and give it more strength and intensity, but to reduce me to the state of an object—I am suddenly "fixed," I become a thing among other things. My body—which is for me the contingent aspect of my situation,[8] the point of view behind which I can no longer seek refuge, the instrument which I cannot utilize by means of any instrument, but around which the world is organized in an ensemble of tools—becomes for the Other an element in an infinite instrumental series, the "perpetual 'outside' of my most intimate 'inside,'" but an outside which "escapes me on all sides." Thus the "shock of the encounter with the Other is for me a revelation in emptiness of the existence of my body outside as an in-itself for the Other,"[9] and at the same time of the alienation of my freedom. For the Other, I am a coward, a hypocrite or just lazy; or if one prefers, honest and generous—just as the table is a table and the inkwell is an inkwell.

We spoke about shame and one might think that it arises only when we are caught in the act of doing something clumsy or awkward, or even more so when we are caught with our eye glued to a keyhole. But the scope of this feeling must be considerably enlarged.

> Pure shame is not a feeling of being this or that guilty object but in general of being *an object*; that is, of *recognizing myself* in this degraded, fixed, and dependent being which I am for the Other. Shame is the feeling of an *original fall*, not because of the fact that I may have committed this or that particular fault but simply that I have 'fallen' into the world in the midst of things and that I need the mediation of the Other in order to be what I am.[10]

The tragic thing here is that I recognize myself in this nature, in this front which the Other confers upon me and reflects back to me. If this were only a purely artificial representation, without any real relation with what I am, it would be of little importance and I would not concern myself with it, for I would certainly not be deeply affected. We must therefore admit that in the presence of the Other, it is a new type of being which reveals itself to me and that "I need the Other to fully grasp the structures of my being," since the for-itself refers me back to the for-others.[11]

This is what Daniel writes to Mathieu, the philosopher in *The Roads to Freedom:*

> Will you understand me, for a start, if I tell you that I have never known what I *am*? My vices, my virtues, are

under my nose, but I can't see them, nor stand far
enough back to view myself as a whole. I seem to be a
sort of flabby mass in which words are engulfed; no
sooner do I name myself than what is named is merged
in him who names, and one gets no farther. . . . For one
instant, on that June evening when I elected to confess
to you, I thought I had encountered myself in your
bewildered eyes. You *saw* me, in your eyes I was solid
and predictable; my acts and moods were the actual consequences of a definite entity. And through me you
knew that entity. I described it to you in my words, I
revealed to you facts unknown to you, which had helped
you to visualize it. And yet you saw it, I merely saw you
seeing it. For one instant you were the heaven-sent
mediator between me and myself. . . . I then understood
that one could not reach oneself except through
another's judgment, another's hatred. And also through
another's love perhaps.[12]

And thus each one of us is in an ambiguous situation:
"I accept and I want the others to confer upon me a being
which I recognize," for shame is an *admission,* just like
pride—which is but a flight reaction (I am proud only to
the extent that I am resigned to be only what one wants
me to be).

But the type of being which is bestowed upon me and
for which I feel responsible, since I am ashamed of it, has
its foundations outside of me. It is beyond the reach of
my freedom, becoming the means toward ends which are
not mine. I am therefore no longer in control of the situation. I do not know "who I am, nor what is my place in the
world, nor what sort of face the world in which I am
is turning toward the Other." The unpredictable freedom of the Other has caught me in its nets and holds me
in bondage.

Under these conditions, the presence of the Other appears as a scandal which I cannot stop, since "surveying" is impossible, which would allow me to escape from the plurality of consciousnesses. All I can do is try to recover the being which has been stolen from me. And thus my look will confront the look of the Other, my freedom will confront his freedom with all the risks this involves. I am therefore compelled to live in an atmosphere of conflict.

This conflict may take on many forms, but the same essential conducts will always be underlying them. When faced with an opponent we wish to disarm, only two attitudes are possible: to seduce him or to break him, which amounts to saying here that we must either capture the freedom of the Other or reduce him to the status of an object.

> In the first case, I am addressing the Other as a subject, I try to seduce him in his transcendence, to persuade him to freely accept me as a limitation to his freedom; I try to make him love me; he will then consider me as a sort of absolute, as a supreme value. In the second case, I address the Other as an object: I try to seize him, to imprison him in his facticity, in his body; I want to appropriate his freedom through a total appropriation of his body.
>
> In short, my phobia is to feel 'alienated' by the Other, not to be able to control this 'outside' which I am for him. My goal is thus either to make the Other valorize my existence by fascinating his freedom to ensure its willing cooperation or to recover my being-for-others by coercing the freedom of the Other, through desire or violence, into acknowledging its defeat.[13]

But we can already say that things will not work out as we would like and that, whichever plan we choose and however hard we try, the conflict of consciousnesses will always remain. There are but two fundamental attitudes in interhuman relations, and we are condemned to allow ourselves to be indefinitely tossed from one to the other.

The Failure of Enterprises of Seduction

First of all, what about love? The lover, we have already seen, strives to become the supreme value of the beloved. "Uneasy about that unjustified, unjustifiable protuberance" of his existence which he feels is "de trop," he wants it to be taken up "in its tiniest details by an absolute freedom which at the same time his existence conditions." He craves its justification. He therefore makes himself appear as a fascinating object. He avails himself of all the resources of language—not only spoken language, but also all the forms of expression which aim at "causing to experience."

And he does this without foreseeing the result. He proceeds "blindly." He cannot conceive what effect his attitudes and gestures will have, "since they will always be taken up and founded by a freedom which will surpass them and since they can have a meaning only if this freedom confers one on them."[14] In this matter, everything depends on the freedom of the Other—on which he is trying to act by a magical process—and not on his own freedom. Success is therefore never guaranteed.

And even if it were, he would never reach the desired goal. We must not forget that to love is to want to be loved, and that under these conditions, the person who responds to our love expects from us what we expect from him. We wanted to be justified through him, he wants to be justified through us. It is a contradictory ideal:

I demand that the Other love me and I do everything possible to realize my project; but if the Other loves me, he radically deceives me by his very love. I demanded of him that he should found my being as a privileged object by maintaining himself as pure subjectivity confronting me; and as soon as he loves me he experiences me as subject and is swallowed up in his objectivity confronting my subjectivity.[15]

Thus relations of love are "a system of indefinite reference" which oblige the lovers to remain in a total subjectivity. It is true—and this is quite an advantage—that as long as I am loved, I no longer feel endangered by the presence of the Other's freedom. But this gain is altogether precarious. All that is needed to destroy it is that the loved one should awaken and contemplate me as an object, or that a third person should look at us together.

And thus love—which is constantly imperilled—is essentially a deception of others and of oneself.[16] It is a self-deception of such a nature that its victim might turn toward masochism. Since love does not succeed in justifying my existence, why not make myself an object before the Other? I will then abdicate my freedom, I will submit willingly to the enslavement imposed upon me. And living my being-for-others in shame, I will love this shame "as the profound sign of my objectivity."

But the masochist is no more successful than the lover. He wanted to surrender his freedom, to engage himself wholly in his being-as-object, to become an instrument for the Other. In fact it is he who uses the Other for his own ends, and "the more he tries to taste his objectivity, the more he will be submerged by the consciousness of his subjectivity—hence his anguish." It is useless for him

> to get down on his knees, to show himself in ridiculous positions, to cause himself to be used as a simple lifeless instrument. It is *for the Other* that he will be obscene or simply passive, for the Other that he will undergo these postures; for himself he is forever condemned *to give them* to himself.[17]

It is therefore impossible to seduce the Other. It would perhaps be better to ignore him and take refuge in indifference; to brush against him as though he did not exist, or more exactly to consider him as a function. He will be the ticket collector or the café waiter, and knowing the keys to their mechanisms, I will use them as suits me best. Indifference is also a sort of "blindness" with respect to others; it is a deliberate blindness, not one that I endure. It can be maintained for a long time, it can last a whole life "save for brief and terrifying flashes of illumination." And it too is failure: not only does "the Other's disappearance as "regard" [look] throw me back into my unjustifiable subjectivity," but "I am in danger without knowing it" and filled with uneasiness "because it is accompanied by the consciousness of a 'wandering and inapprehensible look,' and I am in danger of its alienating me behind my back."[18]

The Other's freedom is always there. I cannot ignore it. And since I can neither ignore nor seduce it, there is only one solution left: to try to conquer it by making it my thing. This is the intention behind sexual desire.

The Failure of Enterprises of Subjection

Desire is an attitude aiming at enchantment. Since I can grasp the Other only in his objective facticity, the problem is to ensnare his freedom within this facticity. It is necessary that it acquire substance as would cream that is being whipped. So the Other's for-itself must come to play on the surface of his body, and be extended all through his body; and by touching this body I should finally touch the Other's free subjectivity. This is the true meaning of the word *possession*. It is certain that I want to *possess* the Other's body, but I want to possess it insofar as it is itself a 'possessed'; that is, insofar as the Other's consciousness is identified with his body,[19]

insofar as it has become incarnate in his body. But there can be no incarnation of the Other without my own incarnation; no ensnarement of his freedom without ensnarement of mine. Reciprocity is necessary.

But when, driven by desire, I try to seize the "saturated" body of the Other, this reciprocal incarnation collapses.

My own body ceases to be flesh and becomes again the synthetic instrument *which I am*. And by the same token, the *Other* ceases to be an incarnation; she becomes once more an instrument in the midst of the world which I apprehend in terms of its situation. Her consciousness, which played on the surface of her flesh and which I tried to *taste* with my flesh, disappears under my sight; she remains no more than an *object* with object-images inside her.[20]

Desire has missed the mark.

It is then that sadism might arise, sadism which is "passion, barrenness, and tenacity." It is still a question of seizing the Other's facticity, but combined with a refusal to be incarnated. It is through violence and pain that the sadist strives to make the Other an instrument and to ensnare him in his flesh. By means of torture he hopes to compel the threatening freedom of the Other to choose to be identified with his "panting and obscene" flesh.

But this odious enterprise is also doomed to failure. The look of the victim—this look which Faulkner portrayed with power in the final pages of *Light in August*—will fix the sadist in his torturer's attitude. The sadist may have forced the Other to humiliate himself, to beg for mercy, but it remains impossible for him to act on his freedom. It is through it, through this absolute and irreducible freedom, "that there exists a world in which there are sadism and instruments of torture and a hundred pretexts for being humiliated and for forswearing oneself." Thus, "this exploration of the Other's look in the world of the sadist causes the meaning and goal of sadism to collapse."[21]

From deception to deception, will we finally reach a solution? Since it has not been possible to gratify the Other's freedom, we try to destroy it. And we then have hate; that is, the project of realizing a world in which the Other does not exist. "I wish to rid myself of the existence that is obsessing me, and not only of the existence of a particular Other but of the existence of all Others." For "what I want to attain symbolically by pursuing the death of a particular Other is the general principle of the existence of others."[22]

It is a senseless project no doubt, but even if it were carried out it would not in any way bring the desired appeasement.

> He who has once been for-others is contaminated in his being for the rest of his days even if the Other should be entirely suppressed; he will never cease to apprehend his dimension of being-for-others as a permanent possi-

bility of his being. He can never recapture what he has alienated; he has even lost all hope of acting on this alienation and turning it to his own advantage since the destroyed Other has carried the key to this alienation along with him to the grave. What I was for the Other is fixed by the Other's death, and I shall irremediably be it in the past. I shall be it also and in the same way in the present if I persevere in the attitude, the projects, and the mode of life which have been judged by the Other. The Other's death constitutes me as an irremediable object exactly as my own death would do.[23]

When, in *The Flies,* King Aegisthus celebrates "the day of the dead" to terrorize the population of Argos, he does it with good reason. It is because the dead are no longer that they remain the guardians of all sins and all crimes.

We are beginning to see that despite a certain variety of expression, the relations between men allow for only two fundamental attitudes: love and hate; and that, tossed from one to the other, we never succeed in escaping the threats of the Other on our freedom. We are caught in an infernal circle from which there is no escape. This is the very situation described in *No Exit.* Unable to resort any longer to the various means of escape (isolation, sleep, silence), or to the deforming processes (lies, hypocrisy) which, during our life, mislead us as to the condition of man, Garcin, Estelle, and Inez are condemned to be both torturers and victims in an endless coexistence.[24]

And the key phrase here might well be "Hell is the others," at least inasmuch as, ensnared in the Other's look and obsessed with his judgment, we seek—in vain and in bad faith—for our justification through him or against him.[25]

NOTES

1. Jean-Paul Sartre, *Being and Nothingness* (New York: Citadel Press, 1966), p. 199.
2. Henry Bergson, "Life and Consciousness," *The Hibbert Journal* X (1911-1912), pp. 24–44; p. 28.
3. Sartre, *op. cit.*, p. 202.
4. Francis Jeanson, *Le Problème Moral et la Pensée de Sartre,* Collection Pensée et civilisation (Paris: 1947), p. 262.
5. Sartre, *op. cit.*, pp. 133–134.
6. *Ibid.*, p. 231.
7. Jean-Paul Sartre, *The Reprieve* (New York: Knopf, 1947), p. 135.
8. Cf. Sartre, *Being and Nothingness,* pp. 284–285: "For human reality, to be is to-be-there; that is, 'there in that chair,' 'there at that table,' . . . It is an ontological necessity." Sartre says:

   > This point must be well understood. For this necessity appears between two contingencies; on the one hand, while it is necessary that I be in the form of being-there, still it is altogether contingent that I be, for I am not the foundation of my being; on the other hand, while it is necessary that I be engaged in this or that point of view, it is contingent that it should be precisely in this view to the exclusion of all others. This twofold contingency which embraces a necessity we have called the *facticity* of the for-itself.
   >
   > And what about the body in this perspective? It might be defined as *the contingent form which is assumed by the necessity of my contingency.* The body is nothing other than the for-itself; it is not an in-itself *in* the for-itself, for in that case it would solidify everything. But it is the fact that the for-itself is not its own foundation, and this fact is expressed by the necessity of existing as an engaged, contingent being among other contingent beings. As such the body is not distinct

from the *situation* of the for-itself since for the for-itself, to exist and to be situated are one and the same; on the other hand the body is identified with the whole world inasmuch as the world is the total situation of the for-itself and the measure of its existence.

9. *Ibid.*, p. 238.
10. *Ibid.*, pp. 264–265.
11. *Ibid.*, p. 277.
12. Sartre, *The Reprieve*, p. 405.
13. Francis Jeanson, *op. cit.*, p. 272.
14. Sartre, *Being and Nothingness*, p. 349.
15. *Ibid.*, p. 352.
16. Cf. Suzanne Lilar, *A propos de Sartre et de l'amour.*
17. Sartre, *Being and Nothingness*, p. 354.
18. *Ibid.*, p. 358.
19. *Ibid.*, p. 370.
20. *Ibid.*, p. 374.
21. *Ibid.*, pp. 381–382.
22. *Ibid.*, p. 387.
23. *Ibid.*, p. 387.
24. Robert Campbell, *Jean-Paul Sartre ou une Littérature Philosophique* (troisième édition), pp. 127–139.
25. Cf. Sartre, Preface to a recording of *No Exit*.

(VIII)

Is Man a Useless Passion?
Atheism

The Other's look and his freedom have condemned us to an atmosphere of perpetual conflict. And this was only a human look. Could there not be another look which would see everything and make everything exist, including ourselves and the whole of mankind? A look to which man would gladly surrender? A look before which the others and I would become this "we," which we sense we are in spite of everything?

We know that when two persons are looking at one another, it is enough that a third appear for the confronting freedoms to blend. But we also know that this experience is done and undone depending on circumstances and on our will. A person can be a third party one moment and not the next. If I turn to look at him, his power collapses; in order for this not to happen, I would have to be dealing with a third person who would be exclusively a third person, an absolute Third person; that is, God.

It Is Pointless to Have Recourse to God

Let God exist, and he will see everything, the others as well as myself, and he will be both our justification and our comfort. This is what believers think. It is also the opinion of Daniel—one of the unhappy characters in *The Roads to Freedom,* when he speaks to God as follows: "Thou hast created me even as I am, and thy purpose is inscrutable; I am the most shameful of thy thoughts, thou seest me and I serve thee. . . . I am thy creature . . . Thou maintainest me . . . Thou seest me, Thou lovest me."[1] And he writes to Mathieu:

God sees me, Mathieu; I feel it and I know it. . . . You must have experienced, in the subway, in the foyer of a theater, or in a train the sudden and irksome sense that you were being looked at from behind. You turn around, but the observer has buried his nose in a book; you can't discover *who* was looking at you. You turn back, but you are sure that the unknown eyes are again upon you. . . . Well, that is what I felt for the first time, on September 26, at three o'clock in the afternoon, in the hotel garden. No one was there, you understand, Mathieu, no one at all. But the look was there. Understand me well: I did not see it, as one sees a passing profile, a forehead, or a pair of eyes; for its essential character is to be *beyond perception.* But I became more compact and concentrated, I was both transparent and opaque. I existed *in the presence* of a look. Since then I have been continually under observation. . . . What anguish to discover that look as a universal medium from which I can't escape! But what a relief as well! I know at last that I am. . . . I need no longer bear the responsibility of my turpid and disintegrating self: he who sees me causes me to be; I am as he sees me. I turn my eternal, shadowed face towards the night, I stand up like a challenge, and I say to God: here I am. Here I am as you see me, as I am. . . . a presence supports me to continue thus forever. . . . Before God and before men, I *am*.[2]

Thus, writes Daniel, God exists. He sees me. And I immediately escape from the uncertainties of my freedom and from the hell into which the Other's look was plunging me. For I now have found this justification I had been seeking in vain. I know that I am and that my life is meaningful. My place is definitively marked out in the world.

But is Daniel right? And if God exists, is he not, instead of a peaceful haven, the most unbearable of all presences? He is a look, certainly, but a look which is impossible to look at, which sees everything but which no one can see. Theologians say that He is eternal and almighty. They might just as well speak of an "inapprehensible look" or of a for-itself which will never be a "for-others," which amounts to saying that with respect to us, He is truly the Other, the inaccessible Other, and that before Him, alienation is total and irremediable.

When I am dealing with the human look, I feel the threat weighing upon me: the enemy is in the fort. But this destruction he brings about, I do not accept; I fight against it. To be sure, I am obliged to recognize the face which the other reflects back to me, for I know that I am this face, but I assume it only to reject it, my being-for-itself refusing to vanish into the for-others and my consciousness refusing to become an object. My freedom confronts that of the Other, my look confronts his look. It is always possible to fight back, even if it will get us nowhere.

But with God, we cannot conceive of any confrontation, and the look then appears as this "universal milieu" from which I cannot escape in any way, since I have no hold on it. The Opponent is inapprehensible and will leave me no peace. "Hell is other people," said Garcin. If God exists, it is even more true that "Hell is God."

But we need not worry, God does not exist. He is but "the concept of the Other carried to the limit." Daniel's impression was but a dream and an illusion. "What trite rambling!" thought Mathieu, upon reading the lucubrations of his friend. Mathieu had already told us what he thinks of war: "War is everywhere, it is the totality of all my thoughts, of all Hitler's words, of all Gomez's acts; but no one is there to add it up. It exists solely for God. But God does not exist."[3]

And it is true that God does not exist. All that we know about man proves it. God and human freedom cannot coexist.

God Does Not and Cannot Exist

Once more we listen to Orestes:

Orestes: You are the king of gods. . . . But you are not the king of man.
Jupiter: Impudent spawn! So I am not your king? Who, then, made you?
Orestes: You. But you blundered; you should not have made me free.
Jupiter: I gave you freedom so that you might serve me.
Orestes: Perhaps. But now it has turned against its giver. And neither you nor I can undo what has been done. . . . What have I to do with you or you with me? We shall glide past each other, like ships in a river, without touch-

ing. You are God and I am free; each of us is alone, and our anguish is akin.[4]

This is a refusal of God, but we must go beyond it, at least beyond the blasphemous form in which it is presented here. Jupiter is a mythological being and is not Orestes' creator. If he were, as believers would have it, this insolent dialog would be meaningless. Orestes could then only affirm his dependence with respect to God and cry out, with his sister Electra: "Jupiter, king of gods and men, my king, take me in your arms, carry me from this place, and shelter me. I will obey your law, I will be your creature and your slave, I will embrace your knees."[5]

Even such an act of submission would be superfluous. What is the use of promising what one is forced to do? A promise makes sense only if there is a free commitment. In the hypothesis of a creator God, there can be no other freedom than his. There can be no rebelling Orestes, no submissive Electra. Man is rigorously determined; he fulfills his destiny. He follows a path that has been laid out beforehand, and realizing the essence which another has chosen for him, he is dependent on him as an object is dependent on the person who first conceived it.

But we know this is precisely not the case. We know that man invents his road and realizes his own project. At the beginning he is nothing. It is he who must make himself and who becomes what he makes himself.

We must therefore acknowledge that if man exists—and he does—God does not exist. Orestes' freedom is Jupiter's death. Can we say even more and go on to a question of rights? Sartre is convinced that we can. For him, even if it were possible to reconcile human freedom with divine freedom—as Descartes claims we can—then we should reject God, for the very notion is contradictory.

What do theologians say? That he is Being in its plenitude and, simultaneously, sovereign freedom. That is, he is both Being and consciousness, which can be translated into Sartrian language by saying that God is an In-itself-For-itself. God is In-itself; that is, identity, coincidence with self, without cracks and without nothingness, "a being who is what he is—in that he is all positivity and the foundation of the world." He is For-itself, that is "self-consciousness and the necessary foundation of himself—a being who is not what he is and who is what he is not." But we immediately see the contradiction. It is blatant and irreducible. God is presented simultaneously as the Being who is and the Being who is not.

How then can we understand the arguments of theologians and philosophers, who delight in referring us from the imperfect to the perfect, who are only too willing to imagine that the idea of God can be the keystone of any well-constructed intellectual edifice? And most of all, how can we understand that such a contradictory notion can, today as yesterday, still obstruct philosophical speculation and continue to haunt the mind of men—ours and even that of Sartre!

It is a fact that consciousness is presence to self, at a distance from self. Since it does not coincide with itself, it carries Nothingness within itself. And it is an unhappy consciousness, since the being which is not what it is and which is what it is not is aspiring toward identity. It dreams of density and plenitude. It wishes this nothingness which is haunting it would disappear from it (if we can use such terms) and wants to become in-itself; not the contingent and "de trop" In-itself which made Roquentin feel nauseous, but an In-Itself which could be termed "essential"—that, for example, of the paper knife or of the statue which, because it preexisted first in the mind of the artist, appears as an indispensable object.

It is in this sense that the imperfect surpasses itself toward the perfect, or (what amounts to the same thing) that the for-itself tends toward the in-itself on condition, however, that we add that this does not mean it will accept opacity and darkness. For if consciousness dreams of being, it refuses to abdicate and to lose itself. It wants to be and yet remain consciousness. Its project is to become "the foundation of its own being-in-itself by the pure consciousness which it would assume of itself."

And this is indeed the In-itself-For-itself of metaphysicians, but it is not the perfect Being of which they speak, the omnipresent creator. It is simply a human value, "The being toward which human reality surpasses itself is not a transcendent God; it is at the heart of human reality; it is only human reality itself as totality."[6]

In other words, man does not tend toward a nonexistent God, but aims at becoming God himself. This is his fundamental aspiration. "God is first 'sensible to the heart' of man as the one who identifies and defines him in his ultimate and fundamental project."[7]

Project, aspiration, desire: this is what the idea of God is expressing. We could also speak of passion, but of a useless passion which strives toward the impossible.

> Every human reality is a passion in that it projects losing itself so as to establish being and by the same stroke to constitute the In-itself which escapes contingency by being its own foundation, the *Ens causa sui,* which religions call God. Thus the passion of man is the

reverse of that of Christ, for man loses himself as man in order that God may be born. But the idea of God is contradictory and we lose ourselves in vain. Man is a useless passion.[8]

But there seems to be a certain danger in saying this. If we say that man is a useless passion, are we not endowing him with an "essence," a "nature" and thus abolishing freedom? Sartre does not think so. It is true that the project of divinization is one of our structures. It is not surprising that an ontology which throws light on our condition should also reveal the secret of our failures and of our disappointments. But we should not confuse condition and nature. Man *is* a useless passion *only* to the extent that he *yields* to his impossible dream.

And besides, is it certain that this passion is the fundamental structure of human reality? Would it not rather be a consequence, the result of historical circumstances which are liable to change? This question does not fall within the scope of ontology but rather of history. It is the latter which will provide the answer.

A New Atheism

In any case, ontological analysis opens up new vistas to atheism and explains an attitude which might appear surprising at first sight. That atheism is an essential given of Sartre's thought, cannot be doubted. We may well be surprised, however, at the use (in order to justify it) of certain arguments which might be more in keeping with a rationalistic system. But what is even more surprising, is the aggressive nature of this atheism. Since God is dead—and he has been dead since Nietzsche—why worry about him? And why those violent and futile invectives in *Le*

Diable et le Bon Dieu? Would it be that he is afraid God might resurrect some day? This is unlikely since Sartre does not hesitate to say that there are only atheists nowadays, since God is dead even in the heart of believers. There must therefore be another reason for this virulent atheism, or else atheism has taken on a meaning different from the usual one.

In reality, in Sartre's view, what is hindering man and paralyzing him most is not the faith he no longer has but his aspiration to Being, to plenitude, his constant referral to an absolute, however it may be conceived. If atheism remains a philosophical conviction, it is above all a practical attitude. It is still the negation of God, but to the extent that the latter is, above all, a symbol. It is therefore a pressing invitation to react against what might be called the theological attitude, "an attempt at secularizing the residue of theology, a permanent conquest of the human over the Transcendent."[9] Again, it is a constant struggle against "the spirit of seriousness which rules over the world," and this spirit we have already discussed[10] is that which Sartre denounces repeatedly and emphatically throughout his work, fustigating the swine and the cowards. The cowards, "because of their spirit of seriousness or of deterministic hypotheses," refuse to acknowledge "their complete freedom." The swine try in vain to believe and to make others believe that their existence is necessary, whereas it is "merely an accident of the appearance of the human race on the earth."[11]

Most people fall into one or the other of these two groups. Let us listen to them. They will often say, as Fred says to Lizzie in *La Putain Respectueuse:* "Who are you? What are you doing in the world? Have you even known your grandfather? Me, I have the right to live. Many things have to be done, and I am being awaited." We recall how Lucien Fleurier and all the dignitaries of Bouville were awaited, as also were those people who, under Roquentin's disapproving look, "are recuperating in order to successfully finish their tasks. Each one of them has his little personal difficulty which keeps him from noticing that he exists; there is not one of them who does not believe himself indispensable to something or someone. . . . Each one of them does one small thing and no one is better qualified than he to do it."[12] He has, so to speak, been commissioned.

They are all victims of the spirit of seriousness or else of a reflection "in collusion" with them, a reflection

> which bears only on the secondary structures of action: it deliberates on the means to reach such and such an end, but refuses to investigate existence or the significance of a supreme end, of a fundamental choice. It is life from day to day, a life which thinks of itself only to justify itself, and which blames itself only for the use of such and such a procedure, and whose fundamental failure can be referred not to a fundamental choice—which one prefers to ignore—but to the fatal nature of all 'destiny.'[13]

There are however a few lucid consciousnesses which rise to a higher level of reflection, to purifying reflection, since "being reveals itself to itself, explicitly, not as chosen by some Fate but as an initial choice of itself, absolutely contingent and unjustifiable."[14] These men refuse to be cowards and swine. By becoming conscious of their contingency and their freedom, they experience the conflict within their being; they feel they have been had—

not by their nature (since there is no such thing), but because of the social conditions and the circumstances in which they live.

On this point, the unhappy story of Jean Genet, told in great detail by Sartre, is significant. A foundling, young Genet has been placed in the care of a family, where he is one day caught stealing. He is ten years old, and an authoritative voice publicly declares: "You are a thief!"

> The metamorphosis occurs immediately. He is nothing more than what he was before, yet he is now unrecognizable. Driven from the lost paradise, exiled from childhood, from the immediate, condemned to see himself, suddenly provided with a monstrous and guilty 'ego,' isolated, separated.[15]

He does not feel guilty but he must be, since everyone thinks he is. Lizzie had said to the persecuted Negro: "All the same, you must be a queer fish to have the whole town after you in this way. . . . They say a Negro has always done something. . . . After all, a whole town cannot be completely wrong." And so Jean Genet is a duped child: "Whatever happens from now on, whatever he may do, whatever way out he may invent, one thing remains forbidden him: *self-acceptance.* The law of his consciousness is conflict."[16]

And what happened so cruelly to Jean Genet, Sartre will depict again in some of his most representative characters. We need only listen to them. For example, in *Le Diable et le Bon Dieu,* Goetz, the bastard, says: "I am made of two halves which do not stick together: each one fills the other with horror." He also makes the following disillusioned comment: "Ever since I was a child, I have been looking at the world through a keyhole: it is a lovely little egg, all full up, where everyone fills the position that has been assigned him. But I can tell you that we are not in it."[17] Out of the family, out of the world: such is the situation.

And Kean, in the play with the same name, is also a bastard. He exclaims violently: "Kean died in the cradle. . . . Shut up, you murderers, it is you who have killed him. It is you who took a child and turned it into a monster."[18] For Goetz and Kean, the law of consciousness has become conflict, as it has, also, for Genet, Roquentin, Orestes, Hugo, and Mathieu. Here we have intellectuals instead of illegitimate children, but they, too, have been duped. They, too, are in a world in which they do not feel at home, for they know what the others do not know. "And I am among them and if they look at me they must think that no one is better qualified than I to do what I'm doing. But *I know*. I don't look like much, but I know I exist and that they exist."[19]

The Difficulties of Atheism

These men, therefore, have also become conscious of the unjustifiable character of their existence. But can we say that they were really successful in this conquest of the human over the Transcendent to which Sartre is inviting us? If we can judge from their attitudes, it would seem not. They are free it is true, but their freedom leads to impotence; it is a freedom for nothing. Just look at them in action.

Orestes wants to be accepted by the people of Argos, and to achieve this he murders Clytemnestra, his mother, and Aegisthus, her lover and the usurper to the throne. But his act is a failure. Argos rejects the son of Agamemnon, who is not one of its own, and prefers servitude to a liberation offered in a magical form, that is, as a spectacle and an example.

Hugo, in *Les Mains Sales,* is a young intellectual full of good intentions and generosity. He too wants to act, hoping thereby to become part of the community of men. He joins the Communist party and, as a token of his sincerity, decides to perform a dangerous mission, a mission he will finally carry out by chance. He kills Hoederer, who is suspected of treason. But his act, far from being the anticipated salvation, turns out to be his condemnation. In a grand gesture, he hands himself over to his executioners. "Unrecoverable!"

During his whole life, Mathieu had the constant care of preserving his freedom of indifference and never committing himself. But this "inexistence" is beginning to weigh upon him. Like the others, he dreams of real action, of accomplishing an irremediable act, and the occasion arises one day in June of 1940. The Germans are entering into the village in which Mathieu and his companions have sought shelter. They refuse to surrender, taking over the steeple and firing indefatigably at the enemy. But the battle is uneven—they fall one after the other. Mathieu has sworn to himself that he will hold out at all cost for fifteen minutes. And he does hold out for fifteen minutes before being killed. The irremediable act has been accomplished, but it is a desperate act.

Antoine Roquentin, more than anyone else, is aware of existence and of its contingency. He knows that he is "de trop" and that everything around him is "de trop," men and things alike. But what conclusions does he draw from this? and what is his attitude? Accusing the others of not knowing, he eyes them with contempt. He will be the just man passing judgment on all others. And breaking away from all others, he betrays society; he is free, but alone. At the same time, in the manner of a schizophreniac, he cuts himself away from the world over which he has no control. But he is still fascinated by it, for he has not found salvation in art.[19]

And thus we see them, these lucid men, these bastards and these intellectuals. They dream of heroic deeds and accomplish only gestures. They are like actors, they only know how to put on a good show. They want to become part of the human community, and they remain desperately alone, traitors almost. They proclaim their freedom and are doomed to impotence. They do not succeed in putting an end to their youth and reaching this age of reason for which they so passionately yearn.

Why is it that the loss of the "spirit of seriousness" ends up in such a failure? And why is it that the thing which should lead to the conquest of the human seems to turn us away from it? Would it be that the task is impossible?

In reality, it is the same malady which paralyzes us all, swine, cowards, and lucid consciousnesses. For in spite of appearances, these failures of freedom are still anxious to be free. Just as in *The Condemned of Altona,* Frantz chose greatness and Johanna chose beauty; they chose lucidity as their end. They wanted *to be* free; that is, to quote Mathieu, "to take only after themselves." Later he says, "Yes free—completely free . . . if I did not try to take up my existence on my own, it would seem to me so absurd to exist." And they who reproach the others with identifying with their facticity, try to identify with their transcendence. Their passion is to be themselves. And thus they reject everything and resort to a freedom which is nothingness:

> This is a consciousness whose fundamental project is to be; it is craving for being, but for being a free consciousness, that is, experiencing the need to feel itself be, to make sure of itself. It tries to satisfy this need by making itself be in the form of nothingness. The result of course is that it misses the being toward which it was aiming.[20]

We should therefore not be surprised at Sartre's bitter comments on his past:

> At the age of thirty, I executed the master-stroke of writing in *Nausea*—quite sincerely, believe me—about the bitter unjustified existence of my fellowmen and of exonerating my own. I *was* Roquentin; I used him to show, without complacency, the texture of my life. At that same time, I was *I*, the elect, chronicler of Hell, a glass and steel photomicroscope peering at my own protoplasmic juices. Later I gaily demonstrated that man is impossible; I was impossible myself and differed from the others only by the mandate to give expression to that impossibility, which was thereby transfigured and became my most personal possibility, the object of my mission, the springboard of my glory. I was a prisoner of that obvious contradiction, but I did not see it, I saw the world through it. Fake to the marrow of my bones and hoodwinked, I joyfully wrote about our unhappy state. Dogmatic though I was, I doubted everything except that I was the elect of doubt. I built with one hand what I destroyed with the other, and I regarded anxiety as the guarantee of my security; I was happy.
> I have changed. . . . The retrospective illusion has been smashed to bits; martyrdom, salvation, and immortality are falling to pieces; the edifice is going to rack

and ruin; I collared the Holy Ghost in the cellar and threw him out; atheism is a cruel and long-range affair: I think I've carried it through. . . .

If I relegate impossible salvation to the proproom, what remains? A whole man, composed of all men and as good as all of them and no better than any.[21]

Man, as he is described by ontology, is simultaneously facticity and transcendence; he must make himself what he is, without reference to any absolute. But is the man of ontology the man of history? This is a last question which we must raise with the *Critique of Dialectical Reason.*

NOTES

1. Jean-Paul Sartre, *The Reprieve* (New York: Knopf, 1947), pp. 208–209.
2. *Ibid.*, pp. 406–407.
3. *Ibid.*, p. 326.
4. Jean-Paul Sartre, *The Flies* (New York: Knopf, 1947), pp. 156–159.
5. *Ibid.*, pp. 161–162.
6. Jean-Paul Sartre, *Being and Nothingness* (New York: Citadel Press, 1966), p. 65.
7. Jean-Paul Sartre, *Existential Psychoanalysis*, translation of several chapters of *L'Etre et le Néant* (New York: Philosophical Library, 1953), p. 66.
8. *Ibid.*, pp. 198–199.
9. Francis Jeanson, *Sartre par lui-même*, (Paris: Editions du Seuil, 1954), p. 171.
10. Cf. Chapters V and VI.
11. Jean-Paul Sartre, *Existentialism and Humanism* (London: Methuen, 1963), p. 52.
12. Jean-Paul Sartre, *Nausea* (New York: New Directions Publishing, 1964), pp. 150–151. Quoted by Francis Jeanson, *op. cit.*, p. 86.
13. Francis Jeanson, *Le Problème Moral et la Pensée de Sartre*, Collection Pensée et Civilisation (Paris, 1947), pp. 291–292.
14. *Ibid.*, p. 293.
15. Jean-Paul Sartre, *Saint Genet: Actor and Martyr* (New York: George Braziller, 1963), p. 18.
16. *Ibid.*, p. 22.
17. Quoted by Jeanson in *Sartre par lui-même*, p. 56.
18. Quoted by Jeanson, *ibid.*, p. 78.
19. Quoted by Jeanson, *ibid.*, p. 86.
20. Cf. Sartre, *Nausea*.
21. Jeanson, *Sartre par lui-même*, p. 130.
22. Jean-Paul Sartre, *The Words* (New York: George Braziller, 1964), pp. 251–255.

(IX)

History Bears out Sartre's Ontology

The *Critique of Dialectical Reason* places man in the context of history—a new perspective, but one which gradually gained credit with Sartre during the Occupation and the years following the war. We see an increasing emphasis in his works on those communities which may be termed "bastard"—the Jews, the Negroes and the Proletariat. For if there are solitary consciousnesses, there are also others—and many of them—whose experience is collective and which are none the less lucid. Just think of the lucidity of the mandarins, and that of the oppressed, which cannot be overlooked. Goetz understood all this, and after his unsuccessful attempts at being God's representative among men, decided to take part in the struggle of the peasants against the barons.[1]

And this evolution, which is quite obvious in *Saint Genet* where it is more a question of *doing* than of *being*,[2] was already part of the development of a philosophy of history. It was also Sartre's encounter with Marxism.

Dialectic

It is true that Sartre had been familiar with Marxism since 1925, when he was but twenty years old. But like most young people of his generation, he had been unable then to grasp its true meaning and import. He was in an ambiguous position as regards this doctrine:

> When we read this philosophy in books, it enjoyed no privilege in our eyes. . . . But when it was presented as a real determination of the Proletariat and as the profound meaning of its acts—for itself and in itself—then Marxism attracted us irresistibly without our knowing it, and it put all our acquired culture out of shape. I repeat, it was not the idea which unsettled us; nor was it the condition of the worker, which we knew abstractly but which we had not experienced. No, it was the two joined together. It was—as we would have said then in our idealist jargon even as we were breaking with idealism—the Proletariat as the incarnation and the vehicle of an idea.[3]

But since then, things have changed considerably. Marxism has assumed its true dimensions for Sartre. Does this mean that he has become an orthodox Marxist—he who only yesterday made no secret of his criticisms of communism? If this were the case, there would be no *Critique of Dialectical Reason* and we would not speak of the Sartrian man. In fact, history opens up new roads, but does not eliminate the givens of ontology. Sartre, unlike the orthodox Marxists of today and perhaps of all times (we are thinking of Engels), strives to maintain man—as he understands him—at the center of dialectic.

Since Hegel, we have known what dialectic is about: contradiction, and search for a totalization. But for Sartre as for Marx, it is not merely a game of ideas and concepts. It is "the living logic of action." It "expresses the real contradictions among men, the concrete negations which are due to the conflict of freedoms; true dialectic unfolds with fists and clubs, with bayonets and cannons: the Marxist 'realism' which Sartre wholeheartedly endorses."

It can also be said that it is not a priori a "construction" but an experience: it is "the very experience of living since living is to act and to endure, and since dialectic is the rationality of the *praxis*." The experience of lacks and needs, of inner and external contradictions, the experience of the willy-nilly overcoming of these contradictions; hence a totalization, but one which is never achieved and is always in progress, "a detotalized totalization."[4]

Now this amounts to saying that dialectic is a human question. It is therefore not surprising that Sartre rejects dialectical materialism which he considers to be a senseless exercise in showmanship and laziness, without the shadow of a proof to back it up, and which might dissolve man into the universe, making him a mere object.[5]

For man is not a thing; he is not "a bag of conditioned reflexes." He is project. "This material being perpetually goes beyond the condition which is made for him; he reveals and determines his situation by transcending it in order to objectify himself—by work, action or gesture,"[6] so that it would be impossible to understand the simplest, the most elementary conduct if one did not bear in mind both the real and present factors which are its condition and the future object which it tends to create.

From the very beginning of history, we encounter man and his project, and history would be impossible if there were not at the very start a dialectical structure of individual action. It is therefore this action which we must describe first, within the context in which it arises. Man, Sartre tells us, is "a practical organism living with a multiplicity of fellow-organisms."[7] He has needs which he must satisfy and he does this through his work. But his work must be carried out in a climate of scarcity.

A Climate of Scarcity and Violence: Alienation

Engels and Marx discussed scarcity at great length, but both of them in ambiguous terms. If we were to take them literally, it would seem that every society has what it needs and that it is the mode of production which, through the institutions it supports, produces the social scarcity of its produce; that is, the inequality of classes.[8]

Now it is not true that every society has all it needs. Scarcity is an unquestionable fact in our modern world. We might well dream—not very convincingly to be sure— of other planets with different living conditions for different organisms. We can also see that at any given time of history scarcity varies from region to region. But how can we overlook the fact that after thousands of years of history three quarters of the population of the world is undernourished and that scarcity is thus "in spite of its contingency, a fundamental human relation (with nature and with men)."[9] Dialectical *praxis* and even work could exist without it. But we certainly would not be the men we are, since we are fundamentally historical creatures. It is not that scarcity is sufficient to produce history—since there are societies which endure a great deal and still have no history. Other factors must be present. But it is scarcity

> on the other hand—as a real and perpetual tension between man and his environment, between man and

man—which *for all intents and purposes* accounts for our fundamental structures [technology and institutions]; not because it would have produced them as an actual force, but because they have been established in a *climate of scarcity* by men whose *praxis* interiorizes this very scarcity in its efforts to overcome it.[10]

For what does scarcity involve? Whatever form it may take, whether it be the shortage of a natural substance, of manufactured products, of men, of time, of space, or of money, it simply means that there is not enough to go around and that all needs cannot be satisfied. I will not be able to consume whatever others have consumed, and the Other becomes a threat. Thus, in all groups there are men who are "de trop," expendable. They are not clearly designated, however. It is possible to determine how many there are, but not who they are. Who will survive: the others, or me? No one knows. Each member of the group is simultaneously a possible survivor and an expendable that should be eliminated—which means that I am a threat to the others, just as the others are a threat to me. And so man, whoever and wherever he may be, becomes the enemy of man. He is the Other, a foreign species, the most dangerous of all. An anti-man, whom one cannot mistrust too much.

And scarcity is now interiorized. It creates a climate of violence since everyone must always and forever be on the defensive. This violence need not necessarily be expressed by action. Engels was right in saying that as action it is absent from many processes. And neither is it a natural feature, a hidden virtuality. It is none of these things but rather

the constant inhumanity of human conducts as interiorized scarcity, in short, that which makes each one of us
see all others as the Other and the principle of Evil. It is
therefore not necessary—in order that the economy
of scarcity become violence—that there be massacres and
imprisonments or any such external show of force. Not
even the actual project of using it. It is enough that the
relation of productivity be established and carried out
in a climate of fear and mutual mistrust by individuals
who are always ready to believe that the Other is an anti-
man and belongs to a foreign species; in other words,
that the Other, whoever he may be, always appears to the
Others as 'the one who started.' This means that scarcity
as the negation through matter of man in man is a principle of dialectical intelligibility.[11]

It is therefore in a climate of violence that the history
of work began and unfolds. The fundamental project of
man is to cast off the mortal danger threatening him and
combat scarcity, in an effort to conquer and overcome it.
It is negation; it must be denied, and this can be done only
through work.

Unfortunately and contrary to our expectations, we see
work turning against man. Whenever an object of con-
sumption or a tool is created, is it not reducing scarcity by
increasing the wealth of the community? And by the same
token, are not the tensions of alterity reducing within the
group? One might expect so, and yet this is not at all how
things happen.

Matter alienates within itself the act which is working
on it, not because it is itself a force, nor even because it
is inertia, but because its inertia allows it to absorb the
work of the others and turn it against each individual.

At the moment of work—that is, at the *human* instant when man objectifies himself by producing his life—the inertia and the material exteriority of the objectivation are such that whatever the human relations may otherwise be, it is the *product* which designates men as Others and which constitutes itself another Species, an anti-man. In order that historical society produce itself through class struggles, it is necessary precisely that *praxis* be detached from this society and restored to men as an independent and hostile reality.[12]

Thus for example, the *praxis* of the Chinese took the form of a material fatality. For centuries they systematically deforested their land to create new plowland; they persistently added destruction to destruction. But they did not see that they were calling misfortune upon themselves, preparing with their own hands what no cataclysm would have been able to do: the floods that would devastate their country.[13]

The demise of Spanish currency during the sixteenth century may be a more complex process, but it is still of the same order. At that time the Mediterranean countries were craving for gold, and since the African source of precious metals had dried up, they turned to America. Spain therefore accumulated gold and silver, ingots and coins, hoping to get rich, or so it thought. For "in spite of strict customs control, in spite of interdicts and police investigations, precious metals are pouring into Spain only to leave it again; gold is leaking through all the borders."[14] Frauds, lawful exports, the imperialistic policies of the government: it all adds up. And, to quote Braudel, Spain is becoming a "water tower" for precious metals. Instead of the anticipated wealth, Spain is getting poorer. And we know why:

All the misadventures of Spanish currency are transformations and reversals of human activity: wherever we
see gold act in such a way as to upset human relations
and this action has been willed by no one, we find underlying this action, a swarm of human enterprises which
aimed at individual or collective goals and which were
metamorphosed through the agency of the thing.[15]

We might make similar reflections for the tool, which
also turns back against man in its own special way. The
tool has a meaning, there is a definite way of using it, and
it is demanding. It is "a *praxis* that has been crystallized
and inverted by the inert which sustains it and, in the tool,
this *praxis* is addressing itself to anyone." A brace or a
wrench indicate me as well as the others. It makes no difference who is using them. Though they indicate the special-
ized worker more directly since it is the group at work
which indicated him, "to the extent that the work of all
depends upon the work of each one," it is in any case the
tool, the machine, which by its structure alone assigns the
task that much be done, so that the *praxis* "does not originate in need or in desire. . . . But inasmuch as it constitutes
itself to reach a foreign objective, it is, in the agent himself, the *praxis* of another and it is another who is objecti-
fied in the result."[16]

Thus matter—that is, matter that is worked upon, since
it is the only one we know—because it is the passive reflection of the *praxis,* becomes counter-finality. The projects
of man are inscribed in it. They are engraved in Being.
And "their translucency changes into opacity, their thin-
ness into thickness, their volatile lightness into permanence; *they become Being* in losing their character of
lived events . . . they refuse, even if they are deciphered
and known, to dissolve into knowledge."[17]

And thus man is constantly engraving his maleficent image into things, but this image leads him astray inasmuch as he allows himself to be fascinated by it. For the practical agent must necessarily recognize himself in the organized inorganic as a material being, as the result of an operation "whether it be a statue, a machine, or his particular interest." He apprehends himself as other than himself. And there lies the explanation of this desire for divinization we already encountered in *Being and Nothingness* and which is at the origin of all our attitudes of bad faith. This fundamental desire which we were tempted to view as a characteristic feature of our nature is now explained by Sartre:

> It is true that *praxis* throws light upon itself, that is, it is always consciousness [of] self. But this non-thetic consciousness is of no avail against the practical affirmation that I am what I have done (which constantly escapes me, immediately constituting me as another). It is the necessity of this fundamental relation which allows us to understand why man projects himself, as I have already said, into the milieu of the In-itself-For-itself.[18]

It is scarcity therefore which makes it possible for us to understand the distressing aspect of history. We now understand why, every moment, man sees "his action stolen and completely distorted by the milieu in which he inscribes this action." We also see why—and from the very beginning—we are in a climate of violence.

The Passive Group

This same climate also prevails within all groups of men, for man lives in society—a society whose form depends on whether its members are passive together or are active together, for, according to Sartre, we must distinguish between the serial group or inert collective, and the group properly so-called.

The serial group can be easily examined by observing a familiar occurrence. Some people are waiting for a bus: men and women of various ages and backgrounds, who are unconcerned with one another. They do not speak to one another, they do not even look at one another. This is a plurality of solitudes, each one of them belonging to a group which is not that of the others. And yet these various individuals form a group. They are on the same sidewalk, at the same bus stop, and have a common interest: they are waiting for the same bus and are all dependent on the vehicle which will soon be coming. Inasmuch as the bus indicates them, they are identical and interchangeable. Their biological or social characteristics are of no importance "inasmuch as they are united by an abstract generality, they are identical as distinct individuals . . . each one is the same as the Others in so far as he is Other than himself."[19]

But there is not enough room on the bus for everyone. Some of them become expendables. But how does each one determine whether or not he falls into that group? Not by his intrinsic qualities but with the help of the ticket he holds; that is, by *the order* of his arrival at the bus stop. This is how conflict and arbitrariness will be avoided. We see thus how "serial unity as being in the common interest becomes a compelling exigency and eliminates all opposition."[20]

But then if "the unity of each one with the other, with all others, never arises in him and in the other as a true relation based on reciprocity," we must admit that it is "ever present but ever elsewhere" and that it is a "unity of flight." It is endured and lived in a state of impotence, for impotence (which in some cases does not exclude violence—though it is then a disorganized violence) characterizes all serial groupings.

Think, for example, of a radio broadcast. My relation with the speaker is not a human relation. Whether I agree or disagree with the voice I am hearing is of no importance; I must remain passive. The speaker has prepared his broadcast in a definite manner. He is addressing me. The voice is *praxis* and, with respect to it, I am an object. It is true that I may change the station if I do not like the broadcast to which I am being subjected. I might even, in a fit of impatience, switch off the set. But this will not prevent the voice from carrying on, from being heard by thousands of people. I denied myself as an individual in the group, but I did not affect the offending voice in any way; it is beyond my reach. And if it is an ideological broadcast which is contrary to my views, however indignant I may become, it is of no avail. For I know that others are listening to what I refuse to hear and that they might be convinced. And sometimes, instead of turning it off, I listen to what is being said, hoping to find fault with it and triumph over it. I then put myself in the place of the others, trying to see what might attract them. I measure the strength of the arguments, and in so doing I partially surrender. I experience a feeling of uneasiness and fascination, since I am simultaneously refusing and allowing myself to be persuaded. In all cases, it is impossible for me to take effective action. I am enduring.[21]

But impotence is not the exclusive property of these inert collectives which are for Sartre the occasion of such brilliant analyses as that of the broadcast we are discussing, or the settling of price-ceilings in a competitive market; it also characterizes the class to the extent that the latter is a serial group. We are dealing then with the "class-being" and not with an active group.

> The class as a collective becomes a material thing made out of men inasmuch as it constitutes itself a negation of man or a serial impossibility of denying this negation. This impossibility makes the class a *de facto* necessity: it is destiny and cannot be altered. It is not a practical solidarity, but, on the contrary, the absolute unity of destinies through lack of solidarity. Each worker feels himself confirmed in his inertia by the inertia of all the others; each little organized group experiences its class as the universal flight which neutralizes its efforts.[22]

Inertia and impotence are therefore the main characteristics of the collective, whatever form it may take. Of course, this group is referred to a *praxis* and a freedom; but it is an endured *praxis,* not an acted *praxis;* it is the product, says Sartre, of an "alienating objectivation."[23]

The Active Group

But this is not the only existing social reality. There is another: the group properly so-called, the active group. Whereas the collective is defined by its being, "the group is defined by its enterprise and by this constant integrating process which aims at making it pure *praxis* by trying to eliminate all form of inertia within it."[24] Materiality has been surpassed and impotence overcome.

How does it all happen? Sartre, as he is wont to do, chooses a striking example and with its help tries to discover the stages of the process which transforms an inert collective into a group. He examines the fusion into a group of the people of Paris during the days preceding the fall of the Bastille.

The people were already extremely restless on the twelfth of July, 1789; but the deep roots of their anger had still only wounded the masses in their common impotence. The pressure of external events is essential to the creation of groups. In this case, we have the electorate assembly in accordance with royal wishes—the resulting representation—the attitude of the government which, from without, will constitute Paris as a totality. "It is necessary," proclaims Louis XVI, "that I make use of my power to restore and maintain power in the capital city. This is why I ordered a gathering of troops around Paris."

Add to this the many rumors, the bits of news, the posters—all constantly creating and maintaining a state of turmoil. People are running and shouting, meeting, and lighting fires. There are incidents between the military and the people, at the town gates and even in the Tuileries gardens. The gunsmiths' shops are plundered; everyone wants to arm. But this is still collective behavior.

> Everyone is determined to arm by the efforts of the Others to find weapons; everyone tries to get there before the Others, since within the context of this new scarcity, the effort of the one to find a gun becomes the danger for the other that he will remain unarmed; at the same time [this conduct] is constituted by relations of imitation and contagion, everyone recognizes himself in the Other by the way he falls into step with him.[25]

We are still in the presence of inorganic groupings, however violent and however effective.

But the group is not far away. The establishment of

militia in the town in order to disperse all crowds and disarm the citizens, was all that was necessary for the group
to discover its reality as being organized. It is then that
Paris experiences what Malraux calls the Apocalypse in
L'Espoir. Serial unity, with its impotence, vanishes into
the group-in-fusion. The latter still has no structures, but
it appears as "the immediate opposite of alterity . . . for
in the serial relation, unity as Reason for the series is
always *elsewhere;* in the Apocalypse, though seriality
remains at least as a process in way of liquidation—and
though it is always liable to reappear—the synthetic unity
is always *here;* or, if you prefer, all the action is taking place in every corner of the town, at every moment,
in every partial process, and the movement of the town
finds its fulfillment and its significance in this action."
Montjoye wrote:

> That evening Paris was a new town. The cannon was
> firing intermittently, warning people to remain on the
> alert. To the sound of the cannon was added that of
> the bells, endlessly ringing the alarm. The sixty churches
> in which the inhabitants had gathered were packed full—
> everyone was an orator. . . . Here the group-in-fusion
> is the town.[26]

It is no longer a serial group but action. The mediator
is not an object here. It is a *praxis:* each individual trying
to integrate his *praxis* into the common *praxis.* Thus

> the essential character of the group-in-fusion is the sud-
> den resurrection of freedom. Not that it ever ceased to
> be the very condition for action and the mask concealing
> alienation, but we have seen that it has become, in the
> practico-inert field, the mode in which the alienated man
> must indefinitely live his imprisonment and finally the

only way he can discover the necessity of his alienation and of his impotence. The explosion of revolt as the elimination of the collective does not *directly* originate in the alienation unveiled by freedom nor from freedom endured as impotence; a set of historical circumstances is necessary, a definite change in the situation, the risk of death, violence . . . but when faced with the common danger freedom wrests itself away from alienation and asserts itself as the common efficacy.[27]

And each individual assumes a new dimension. He still sees himself through the eyes of the others, as an object, but "in a lived objectivity." He is no longer the Other "who comes to the others while doing a disservice to himself by his mere physical presence." He is his own action in the group *praxis*.[28]

And thus we see freedom wrenching away from alienation in the group-in-fusion and asserting itself as the common efficacy. But this is in violence and in the face of danger. What will happen when the threat is removed or even *seems* to be removed? Will the group survive? And what are the conditions for this survival?

The first statute of the group is the oath. Threatened by seriality and dispersion, the group will create a fake inertia which will protect it from real inertia. Whether it be an explicit oath (the *Serment du Jeu de Paume* for instance) or whether it be "the implicit assumption of the oath as an already existing reality of the group (by those who are born in the group for instance, and who grow up among its members)," the oath is the promise of a future.

It is both a slogan to enflame the others and "a maneuver against myself. . . . To swear is to give what one does not have so that the others will give it to you and so that one will be able to keep one's word."[29] It is a guarantee against my freedom by means of the freedom of the others. The oath shields me from a possible treason and the exact wording of an oath should not be "I swear" but rather "Let us swear."

It originates in fear of the other and of oneself, for the external fear in the face of danger has been replaced by the inner fear of serial dissolution. The group then exerts pressure upon its members and "the communal freedom creates itself as Terror: the power of life and death is now the stature of the group. . . . The Other is protected against my free treason by this right which I granted to all (and to him) to eliminate me in the event of my failing him, and by the terror which this common right creates within me—this common right which I myself demanded."[30] Anyone who takes an oath is demanding to be defended against himself and accepts beforehand the sentence that will condemn him should he ever turn traitor.

And this is how we become brothers, not because of an identical nature but because we are accomplices in the same act. We are brothers inasmuch as after the creating act of the oath we are *our own sons,* our common invention, "and that we all have rights, each one of us over everybody else." This is violence-fraternity, terror-fraternity, which, in the event of treason, is the practical bond of love uniting the lynchers and also the lynchers and their victim "in the sense that the elimination of the traitor is founded on the positive affirmation that he is *a member of the group.*"[31] We must therefore finally acknowledge that "all *inner conducts of the common indi-*

vidual (fraternity, love, friendship, as well as anger and lynching) derive their terrible power from Terror itself."[32]

In *Being and Nothingness* the scandal seemed to reside in the mere existence of the Other. In fact, as Jean Lacroix pointed out, it is "in endured or threatening violence, in internalized scarcity." And human relations now become intelligible: "By fighting against the enemy, I identify with him in a sense: I understand the *praxis* of the other from within through the action which I produce to defend myself against it. Understanding is an immediate fact of reciprocity."[33]

The Restoration of Constraints

But we also see that the group-in-fusion has become a group-in-constraint. And this movement will continue, but in such a way that inertia will reappear.

In order to ensure its permanence, the group—which was at first a diffuse power of jurisdiction—will become an organization. Duties will be handed out and functions determined: the fluid homogeneity of fusion will be replaced by differentiation. And through the force of circumstances, alterity will crop up again within the group. It is true that the members will remain equivalent, differing only in their functions, for if the group re-internalizes alterity it is only to better be able to fight against it; everything happens as though it produced at such and such a place the strength or the brains which it needs there. But with the oath, and even more so with the function,

> reciprocity is centrifugal: instead of being a lived concrete tie created by the presence of two men . . . it

becomes *the tie of their absence:* each one in his solitude, or amidst the subgroup, derives his guarantees and
his imperatives from the qualification in inertia of common individuals he no longer sees.[34]

The same is true of the institution. Realized by individuals produced by the group, it presupposes powers,
material localization and instrumentality, and involves
a right-duty system. But its true being and its strength do
not derive directly from freedom. They proceed "from
emptiness, from separation, from inertia and from serial
alterity." The institution is *"praxis* inasmuch as it is
other."

> Whether it be an inner *praxis* of organization, of corre-
> lation, of control, a definite struggle against scarcity
> within the group (scarcity of men, of funds, of com-
> munication), in a word whether it be integrating or
> whether it be a duty of the common and transcendent
> action on the object or on the enemy—*praxis* becomes
> an institution that very day when the group, as a unit
> undermined by alterity, is powerless to change it with-
> out completely upsetting itself, that is, the day when
> each one finds himself conditioned by the flight in
> circles of the others.[35]

We are then faced with a process which is not *free
praxis.* It may be dialectical, just as free *praxis* would be;
it has a movement and a direction, triumphing over the
obstacles of the common field and transforming them
into relays, into stages, into steps which mark and facili-
tate their development. It is also "violence, fatigue, wear
and perpetual transmutation of energy." But while free
praxis, in the face of need or danger, invents its own law,
unveiling itself immediately through its project and its

end, this process receives its modification from passivity. "The movement which animates it is not one of those which I can produce, as a practical organism; it falls into the category of those which I endure as having my being-outside-myself in the world."[36] We have gone from free activity to inertia.

The same thing happens with sovereignty. Sovereignty in itself is no problem; it requires no foundation. It is

> man himself as action . . . as having a hold on the world and changing it. Man is *sovereign.* And to the extent that the material field is also the social field, the sovereignty of the individual extends infinitely to all individuals. . . . The only limitation to the sovereignty of man on all others is pure reciprocity, that is, the complete sovereignty of all and everyone over him.[37]

But then sovereignty becomes a function, it depends only very loosely upon freedom. The role of authority, whether it be exercised by one or by many, is then to fight against "the invasion of the group by seriality." It is required by the being of institutions in their internal unity. And things happen as follows: the sovereign founds his authority on serial impotence, he exploits the inertia of internal relations to endow the group with maximal efficiency without, so that his power is not founded on acceptance (as a positive act of adherence) but so that acceptance of his power is an internalization of the impossibility of rejecting it.

Thus we see that for Sartre—and this is what he terms "the locus of history"—the two poles of social dialectic are the object-group and the subject-group; on the one side the *inert collective,* lived in impotence, and on the other *praxis,* which is both individual and common freedom.

But what is important here is that the man of dialectic is not essentially different from the man of ontology.

Consciousness remains the subject of history, and freedom is always underlying human *praxis*. Freedom is indeed primordial and it can even be said that it founds servitude, since alienation exists only if man is first of all action. "If history escapes me," says Sartre, "it is not because I do not make it, but because the Other is making it also."[38]

It is true that we are living under the yoke of scarcity, which is the source of violence, and that the reign of freedom can truly begin only when our present historical condition is eliminated. But does this mean that there are two sorts of freedoms? One is authentic, which we cannot imagine as long as there does not exist "for everyone, a margin of real freedom."[39] The other is that which we know, and which is not true freedom since it is impotent.

In fact, it would seem that for Sartre man is always free, because he is consciousness. But he "must make himself what he is" and acquire this "margin of real freedom" of which he speaks. He must struggle against scarcity and the alienation which is its consequence. Now this struggle depends, in its very source, on the impetus of an authentic freedom, the only force which can counterbalance history.[40] But will it ever succeed, if it is what we are told? Freedom, as ontology and history have revealed it, is sovereign. Not only over its choice, but also over the reason for its choice. It has therefore no mooring point which would give a meaning to its activities. Under such conditions, why should it try to "recuperate itself"? And even if the historical situation were to change, what reason is there for freedom to become its own end? Is it not irremediably condemned to remain a freedom for nothing?

But we are now in a position to ask if Sartre's conception of freedom is acceptable and, by the same token, if his conception of human reality is, also.

NOTES

1. Cf. Jean-Paul Sartre, *Le Diable et le Bon Dieu* (Paris: Gallimard, 1951).
2. Francis Jeanson, *Sartre par lui-même* (Paris: Editions du Seuil, 1954), p. 143.
3. Jean-Paul Sartre, *The Problem of Method*, translation of the prefatory essay in *Critique de la Raison Dialectique* (New York: Knopf, 1963), p. 18.
4. J.-M. Le Blond, "Histoire et Liberté selon Sartre," *Etudes*, Juillet-août, p. 64.
5. R. Garaudy, *Perspectives de l'Homme*, Bibliotheque de philosophie contemporaine (Paris, 1960), p. 122. Cf. *Tribune Libre*.
6. Sartre, *The Problem of Method*, p. 150.
7. Jean-Paul Sartre, *Critique de la Raison Dialectique* (Paris: Gallimard, 1960), p. 668.
8. *Ibid.*, p. 219.
9. *Ibid.*, p. 201.
10. *Ibid.*, p. 204.
11. *Ibid.*, pp. 221–222.
12. *Ibid.*, p. 223.
13. *Ibid.*, pp. 232 *et seq.*
14. *Ibid.*, p. 240.
15. *Ibid.*, p. 249.
16. *Ibid.*, pp. 252–253.
17. *Ibid.*, p. 246.
18. *Ibid.*, p. 86, note.
19. *Ibid.*, p. 311.
20. *Ibid.*, p. 312.
21. *Ibid.*, pp. 320–323.
22. *Ibid.*, p. 353.
23. J.-M. Le Blond, "Histoire et Liberté selon Sartre," p. 67.
24. Sartre, *op. cit.*, p. 307.

25. *Ibid.*, p. 389.
26. *Ibid.*, p. 391.
27. *Ibid.*, p. 425.
28. *Ibid.*, pp. 406–407.
29. *Ibid.*, p. 445.
30. *Ibid.*, p. 450.
31. *Ibid.*, pp 453–455.
32. *Ibid.*, p. 455.
33. Jean Lacroix, *Le Monde*, Nov. 4, 1960.
34. Sartre, *op. cit.*, pp. 476–479.
35. *Ibid.*, pp. 582–583.
36. *Ibid.*, p. 543.
37. *Ibid.*, p. 588.
38. Sartre, *The Problem of Method*, p. 88.
39. *Ibid.*, p. 34.
40. J. Guérémy, *Cahiers de l'Institut de Science Economique Appliquée*, no. 111, March 1961, pp. 101–107.

(X)

Are Sartre's Refusals Legitimate?

Now that our study is coming to an end, we must acknowledge that

> from beginning to end, the philosophical thought of Sartre maintains a remarkable unity and permanence throughout all his works: this permanence is displayed by his repeated affirmation that consciousness is not a thing, that the distinctive feature of human reality is to always surpass itself toward its end, and therefore that it cannot be reduced to the level of determinism.[1]

We make ourselves what we are, in terms of a chosen end and according to a project which is always a surpassing of the given. In other words, man "*is* only to the extent that he exists and he exists [Ex-siste] only by projecting himself toward, he *is* only by being elsewhere, outside-of-himself-in-the-world, he is, in a sense, this impossibility of being oneself. I *am* never in myself, I have no consistency of being within me, I exist only in my relation to the world."[2] And thus, according to Sartre, there is no such thing as human nature; only our freedom exists.

To be sure, this freedom is utterly impotent in the historical conditions in which we are immersed, but it is real, manifesting itself in the most varied attitudes: in our actions which may appear to be spontaneous or purely automatic, as well as in our deliberate choices. And this freedom is always creating values, creating all values. It would be impossible for things to be otherwise. For Sartre it is not a simple matter of fact, but of right. On this point, we must refer to an important text—his study of Descartes, which Henry Duméry considers as the key to Sartrian existentialism.[3]

Among all philosophers, Sartre tells us, Descartes has the keenest sense of the autonomy of man; but he is a mathematician, and it is when faced with intelligible essences that he first proclaims his belief in freedom.

For anything to be true, it is necessary that I affirm it. It is therefore I who am responsible for it, and by the same token, for the order of all truths which appear in the world. It is therefore not surprising that Descartes, when viewing the concatenation of essences, should constantly experience both his freedom and his solitude. "Heidegger said, 'No one can die for me.' But before him Descartes had said, 'No one can understand for me.' We finally have to say yes or no, and decide the meaning of truth for the entire universe. Now this is an absolute and metaphysical act,"[4] an act which displays our resemblance with God—for we are no longer dealing with Descartes alone, but with all of us, who are free.

However, if this is the profound thought of the philosopher, we must admit that circumstances will force it to assume another form and another meaning. What had first been conceived as creation becomes pure adherence.

Descartes believes in the existence of God. Now if God exists, it is clear that there is a preestablished order and that the relations uniting all essences have been fixed by Him and not by man. Under these conditions, what can we do but acknowledge and adhere to what already is, since the will cannot help submitting to the obvious.

But can we still speak of freedom? Descartes does, but not in the same sense as he did at first.

> We had termed 'freedom' the possibility for the will to determine itself, to say Yes or No to the ideas conceived by our understanding, which amounts to saying that the die was never cast, that the future could never be predicted; whereas now, the relations between reason and will, when faced with the obvious, are conceived in the form of a rigorous law for which the clarity and the distinction of the idea are the determining factors toward affirmation.[5]

We were first discussing freedom of indifference. Now, as for Spinoza and Leibniz, we are dealing with the acceptance of necessity and hence with a freedom without free will—and not only in the realm of thought where Truth is constraining our will, but also in matters of Ethics where it is bound by the Good. Descartes wrote to his friend Mersenne:

> You do not agree with me when I say that *it is enough to judge well in order to act well,* and yet it seems to me that the ordinary doctrine of the School is that *voluntas non fertur in malum nisi quatenus ei sub aliqua ratione boni repraesentatur ab intellectu,* whence the phrase *omnis peccans est ignorans,* so that if reason

never presented anything as good which is in fact not good, the will could never make the wrong choice.[6]

Thus, Sartre points out, the Cartesian thesis is now complete, embracing both knowledge and behavior, science and morals.

A clear vision of the Good brings about action as the apprehension of the True brings about agreement, for the Good and the True are one and the same thing, to wit Being. And if Descartes can say that we are never so free as when we do what is Good, it is because he substitutes a definition of freedom in terms of the value of the act—by which the freest of all acts is that which conforms most with the universal order—for a definition in terms of autonomy.[7]

But this is no longer real freedom. The Cartesian man is like the Christian: God leads them by the hand "toward the Knowledge and the Virtue he has chosen for them; they have only to let themselves go and not interfere with the plans of the sovereign will which is guiding them." Moreover, when they do interfere, it is because they do not see or do not see well. Freedom for them is not a creative power, it is simply the negation of what is not, the negation of nonbeing; so that when being appears, freedom is compelled to signify its adhesion to it.

And the conclusion is obvious: we are free only if we invent our own reasons and values, taking thus the place of God, this God who is, as Descartes sees him, "a pure Action, a pure Efficiency, or Liberty, higher than the whole order of intellect or intelligibility, positing itself without reason, by virtue of its power alone, and arbitrarily creating intelligibles and essences."[8] We must try to recuperate this creative freedom which Descartes sees in God, so that man can become "the being whose appearance causes a world to exist." Only then—like Orestes confronting Jupiter—will we be autonomous and truly men.

It would seem therefore, as H. Duméry said, that "the intention of depriving the Cartesian God of his creative freedom in order to bestow it onto man instead" lies at the core of Sartrian existentialism. But will we follow Sartre in this daring enterprise and recognize no true freedom save in the creation of reasons and values? Is this the price of the autonomy of man? The arguments adduced to convince us only succeed in making us more skeptical.

Freedom Presuppose Knowledge of the Good

There is little doubt that we cannot see clearly what Good is without doing it. Most philosophers have acknowledged this, but we must be more precise in our statements; it is not sufficient to speak of inclinations and of Good. We must also know of what Good and which inclinations we are speaking. There seems to be no better guide than Thomism in these matters. Jacques Maritain writes:

> For St. Thomas the will is an appetite, a power of desire and inclination, creating spiritual weights in the soul which attract it completely. Its primordial act is to love.
>
> Now all appetites are rooted in knowledge. What the scholastics called the appetite of the senses—the powers of desire and emotion, which are common to both men and animals—has its roots in sensible knowledge.
>
> Now the will on the contrary, the power of spiritual appetition, is rooted in intelligence. And it is because intelligence has the concept of what is good, defined in its own objective and in its concrete universality, and as

simple as that of being, it is because of this that there must exist in all natures endowed with intelligence a power of desire and love which is essentially distinct from the sensible appetite and which aims toward the Good, known as Good, inasmuch as it transcendentally impregnates all good things and befits the subject, the intelligently apprehended Good and not only certain particular good things apprehended by the senses.[9]

We now understand the nature of this Good which attracts us so irresistibly and from which it would be impossible to withdraw if it were presented to our intuition, since it would eliminate our freedom of choice. This is Sartre's Good, the absolute Good which satisfies all our capacities for desire to the point of saturation, opening up for us this state which many philosophers, both ancient and modern, call beatitude.

But can we really say that this Good ever appears to us in a beatifying intuition? It would most certainly be ridiculous to make such a claim, for we know only particular goods.

These goods are extremely precarious, so that—to use an expression by Merleau-Ponty—they always leave us a "possibility of withdrawal," even with respect to the representation of the absolute Good.

As long as we do not see God face to face, in a beatific vision, our reason and our faith may well tell us that he is the absolute Good and our ultimate end, it still remains that we do not yet possess this beatitude, our intelligence does not apprehend God as the beatitude which is actively beatifying us, it knows him with an abstract knowledge as the beatitude which will beatify us someday. And there are many apparent or real goods

which we will have to give up for the present in order
to reach God; many good and desirable things, which
remain attractive in themselves, outside the narrow path
of those goods which are better for us and which are
oriented toward God, the head of the moral order.[10]

And thus, it is precisely because the will is necessarily
determined toward the absolute Good that it remains indetermined "with no natural and necessary propensities" as
regards particular goods, and retains its freedom of choice.
And we reach this paradoxical conclusion: what Sartre
considered as an unsurmountable obstacle to freedom
appears to us as its very condition.

The indetermination in question is not the "potential
and passive" indetermination of "that which can, since it
is imperfect and awaiting a determination, become this
or that, receive this or that actuation." It is an "active and
dominating" determination so that "freedom consists of
the will's control over that very practical judgment which
determines it."

The free act appears as the common fruit of intelligence and of the will, vitally enveloping one another
in a single and identical instantaneous codetermination:
intelligence determining the will in the order of objective or extrinsic formal causality, the will determining
intelligence in the order of efficient causality; in other
words, specification (by intelligence) is dependent on
exercise (of the will). As for the judgment which, when
effectively carried out, specifies and determines the act
of the will, it is this same will which gives it its value of
existential efficacy, discharging—so to speak—upon the
particular good in question the surplus with which its
determination by the infinite good is making it flow

over. To be free is to be master of one's judgment; the will controls the very judgment which determines it and this is how it has full control over its actions.[11]

Now, if the process we are trying to describe is true (however mysterious it may be); if it corresponds to reality as experience presents it to us, it is obvious we cannot accept Sartre's view of man. The most positive contribution of his phenomenological descriptions must then be inscribed in a context different from his own.

First of all—and this is merely a consequence of what we have just said—the existence of values does not abolish the exercise of freedom. The ethic universal does not destroy moral consciousness. Since the will controls our judgment, no rule, no law, no advice will be able to interfere with our power to make decisions. Whether we be faced with conflicting duties—like the young man described by Sartre, who, under the German Occupation, debated whether he should stay with his mother who needed him or serve his country by joining the Resistance —or whether we are dealing with some simple and indisputable command such as not to kill or not to steal, there is always a choice that must be made, a choice that will be our choice and from which no one, absolutely no one, can exempt us.

Sartre is therefore right—and this will never be sufficiently emphasized—to affirm that no man can relinquish his responsibility and that it is cowardly to even try to do it. The most violent admonitions need not worry us in this domain inasmuch as they fustigate desertion. For it is true that the man who is obeying the law as a slave, as a believer, or as a friend, remains in all cases fully responsible for his act; the latter bursting forth from his own self—unique and unpredictable. And if it were true, as we are told, that it is anguish which reveals freedom, we would have to acknowledge that this feeling is not the apanage of the Sartrian man. The Christian and the sage are well acquainted with it also, and perhaps in an even more tragic manner. In any case, it is not the fact of accepting the law which makes us cowards or swine.

But will we go so far as to say that man is free in all cases, and completely so? Since freedom is not a pure spontaneity of questionable origin, since it presupposes the will and its active and dominating indetermination, it is clear that it does not express itself through all the attitudes of consciousness. This is not a question of all or nothing, and hence of a choice between enslavement and freedom. We are neither always nor completely free; free through and through.

In man, existence does not precede essence, as Sartre would have it, at least not in the sense that existence would actuate nothing that pre-exists it. I would exist, but I would be nothing; man would exist, but there would be no human nature. It is true that we make ourselves through our choices and this is why we are responsible for ourselves. But we do not make ourselves anything we please. We are men and must remain men. As Amiel said, "Man is but what he becomes—this is a profound truth. Man becomes only what he is—an even more profound truth." To think otherwise would be to flounder into the unintelligible.

In fact, we must always speak of human nature, at least in *an analogic sense,* as St. Thomas did, following Aristotle.

Man, as spirit, is essentially 'open' before an unlimited horizon or possibilities! In a sense, he can become all things.

He therefore possesses a native 'plasticity' which unfolds during the course of history in the various solutions offered by cultures and civilizations. Human nature explores thus all its possibilities, all of which are variations on the same basic structure which occurs everywhere and allows sociology and anthropology to have their own object: man as seen through culture and history. In this sense, human nature is of necessity historical.

Moreover, far from opposing freedom as a pure natural given confronting it, human nature, as St. Thomas understands it, includes freedom within itself, and indeed, freedom is its essential property. There is therefore not only a reconciliation of nature and freedom, but integration of the latter into the first. Man is free because his nature is spiritual, because he emerges above those beings which are only nature. Capable of reflection, of introspection, he is an interiority, he is made to possess himself, 'to keep himself in check,' to behave. He then becomes a hotbed of spiritual life which cannot be threatened from without since he can only surrender through a free gift of himself over which he retains full control.[12]

And thus the subjectivity which we are is not an absurd abyss of pure and shapeless freedom. This leaves us quite a distance away from Sartre. And it is not all!

Sartre Refuses the Good

Sartre felt he had to choose between Good and freedom. He rejected the Good, but this refusal was related to another more fundamental one which we must now examine: the refusal of Being.

In *Being and Nothingness,* as he had already done in *Nausea,* Sartre speaks to us first about Being, and in such terms that it is easy to foretell that it will not be consciousness.

Being is the *In-itself,* opaque and solid, a sort of amorphous and indifferent object. It is therefore obvious that consciousness, the *For-itself* which questions and doubts, which remembers and imagines, can exist only if it wrenches itself away from the positivity of being. It is obvious that any authentically human act will consist exclusively of a nihilating withdrawal, which presupposes freedom—the latter being merely the possibility for the for-itself "to secrete a nothingness which isolates it"—so that the anguish which reveals it is "the apprehension of the for-itself, as it exists as a mode of perpetual breaking away from that which is."

Being, the in-itself, always lies at the horizon, as the threat which must forever be eluded. Sartre resorts to countless images to convey the nature of this threat. It is the vague, the amorphous, the flaccid, the tepid, the suspicious, the monstrous, the obscene, the slimy. The slimy most of all; this image—better than any other—makes us grasp what the dreadful hold of the in-itself represents for each one of us. Slime is the agony of water; it does not flow, but draws itself out, levels out, flattens itself out. If you touch it, it does not flee, it yields, it is compressible; and yet when you believe you possess it, it possesses you. It is leech-like. You want to let go of it and it sticks to your fingers. It draws you, it sucks at you. On feeling it, you experience a sort of dizziness.[13]

We said that the for-itself is wrenching away and with-drawal. We might add that it is disglueing. In any case, it exists only to the extent that it is a refusal of Being. And things have to be this way.

Ricoeur is right in affirming that "If Sartre was able to perform a sort of hypostasis of the nihilating act into actual nothingness, it is because he had previously driven Being back to the given, to the world without and within me." His philosophy of being dominates his philosophy of nothingness, and by the same token, his theory of value.

> If being is the brute given, value—which airs the given in a sense, which introduces the 'about to be' into being —cannot but be lacuna and lack . . . . being can no longer be a refuge but a trap; slime, not impulse and foundation. Value must derive its being from its exigency and not its exigency from its being, and we end up having to rely on the nothingness of freedom to make values exist as values.[14]

When the concept of the in-itself has been completely constructed after the model of the thing, it is certain that consciousness will not be, or that it will be nonbeing, that is, non-thing. But why this reduction?

It all began with an intuition which we believe to be genuine. Existence as revealed in *Nausea* is not an "empty form," an "abstract category" allowing us only to think in terms of belonging. "I was telling myself that the sea belonged to the class of green objects, or that the green was a part of the quality of the sea." Now this is not existence. Existence is not the *de-realized being* of logic. And neither is it the *vague being* of common sense, nor the *particularized being* of the sciences.[15] It is the very basis of things, the common source where all comes to life —existence always and everywhere, without limits. It is the act of being, the Thomist *actus essendi*.

But this illumination with which Sartre, aided by the most expressive language, is trying to convey the experience, suddenly opens up onto an overwhelming truth. This is an extasis, but as Gilson says, "a downward extasis." We are faced with "soft, monstrous masses . . . naked, in a frightful, obscene nakedness. . . . I knew it was the World, the naked World suddenly revealing itself, and I choked with rage at this gross, absurd being." For it is of absurdity we must speak. Everything is there for no reason, without point of reference, there is nothing for reason to cling on to. Everything is "de trop."[16]

We are in the presence of opacity, an unsurmountable opacity. And the consequence is obvious: we can say nothing about this being, save that it is.

Ontology therefore is not a science. It will not seek to explain, since intuition brought us in the presence of the absurd, in the presence of a brute given which has no meaning and cannot have any. It will confine itself to the description of phenomena. In this connection, Albert Camus once wrote: "To describe, this is the ultimate ambition of the absurd thought. To contemplate and reproduce the ever virgin landscape of phenomena."

The Rejection of All Metaphysics

And thus ontology, extending psychology, will study the relations of consciousness with being. It will be "the explication of the structures of the existing being considered in its totality." It is therefore phenomenological and not metaphysical.[17] We still speak of being, but it is the being of phenomena, and the in-itself has become—to use an apparently contradictory expression *the transphenomenal being* of phenomena.

It is true that Sartre occasionally mentions metaphysics, but it is always to invalidate its claims. First of all, some of the problems it examines are utterly meaningless, such as the origin of being and of the world. Sartre cuts short any attempts at an explanation:

> You couldn't even wonder where all that sprang from, or how it was that a world came into existence, rather than nothingness. It didn't make sense, the World was everywhere, in front, behind. There had been nothing *before* it. Nothing. There had never been a moment in which it could not have existed. That was what worried me: of course there was a reason for this flowing larva to exist. *But it was impossible* for it not to exist. It was unthinkable: to imagine nothingness you had to be there already, in the midst of the World, eyes wide open and alive; nothingness was only an idea in my head, an existing idea floating in this immensity; this nothingness had not come *before* existence, it was an existence like any other and appeared after many others.[18]

The question of the origin of being is therefore meaningless, but there are other meaningful and legitimate questions which fall within the realm of metaphysics. One might for instance inquire into the origin of the For-itself and also if consciousness is not bound to the In-itself by an internal relation—we might ask how action is possible since "it involves a project which has an immanent origin and which determines a modification in the being of the transcendent."[19]

These are, Sartre tells us, three metaphysical questions which have not yet been answered, though it is not impossible that they will be some day. But, from our point of view it is of little importance whether there is an answer or not, since we are warned that certainty is possible only for the immediate givens of phenomenology, and that metaphysics will therefore never be able to do more than formulate hypotheses, which will be neither validated nor invalidated—their only value being that they help to unify the givens of ontology, which amounts to saying that we will always be the prisoners of our experience, faced with a reality which we will neither be able to understand nor to reduce. Such would be the consequence of our initial intuition.

Contingency Compels Us to Have Recourse to the Necessary Being

On closer examination, we are not certain that the above conclusion is that obvious. We are not certain at all that from the very beginning, dialectic did not encroach upon intuition, to the point of spoiling everything.

There is, on this point, a particularly important text which will guide our reasoning. It is that in which Sartre discloses his first impression when brought face to face with being.

The essential thing is contingency. I mean that one cannot define existence as necessity. To exist is simply *to be there*; those who exist let themselves be encountered, but you can never deduce anything from them. I believe there are people who have understood this. Only they tried to overcome this contingency by inventing a necessary causal being. But no necessary being can explain existence: contingency is not a delusion, a probability which can be dissipated; it is the absolute, consequently the perfect free gift.[20]

Now we see two affirmations here which have neither the same origin nor the same value. The first is presented as the result of an intuition and we will not dispute it. Together with Sartre, we will acknowledge that the existents are contingent and that they do not carry their justification within them—that one encounters them and can deduce nothing from them, so that contingency is not a delusion, a probability that can be dissipated.

But to deny the existence of a necessary Being on the strength of this is to stretch experience quite a bit. And in these questions, it is not enough to affirm.[21] One would have to establish that to explain is always to deduce and that consequently to accept the absolute would be to negate contingency.

In any event, there are people (to use Sartre's words) who do not think this is the case. They have recourse to a necessary Being, without believing for that matter that they will be able to deduce the existents from it and thus surmount contingency. For them

it is the very intuition of Being which allows, supports and surrounds the shock of contingency. What appears as a scandal—all the more felt in the light of the exigencies set by Being itself—is in fact the springboard of the spirit toward the absolute. Without this experienced contradiction, the spirit would have stopped at the dazzling sight of the first glimmers of light. It is the dark lightning of contingency which guides it on the road to the source. And hence the possibility of a metaphysical progress toward the absolute is dependent on the apprehension of contingency within the apprehension of being.[22]

Creation

It is true that in this view of things we must have recourse to creation in order to understand the existent. Now Sartre does not feel this is a solution. On the contrary. He considered this hypothesis but promptly rejected it, feeling it to be utterly useless, even if it were possible. We know the dilemma.[23]

Either the created being is posited by God in an instantaneous act, confronting Him from outside His subjectivity and, closing up upon himself, it becomes its own foundation without retaining the slightest trace of creation. Or else it remains dependent upon the Creator, emanating from the divine consciousness, and, since it has no being of its own, it cannot be distinct from the necessary Being.

In the first case contingency remains and God is of no use in explaining it, since the fissure between Him and the world is irremediable. In the second case, contingency is overcome, but the world, which is no longer distinct from divine thought, has disappeared by the same token—and our intuition of the existent does not allow us to accept this.

Thus creation, if there is a creation, would not solve the problem. It would abandon us without any means of defense, without the slightest possibility of an explanation, in the presence of contingency which is indeed the absolute, the perfect free gift. But we can only accept this if creation is really what Sartre says it is; and we find it hard to believe him on this point.

We do not see how a created being can be independent of the Creator and become its own foundation. That this may be true of human creations—of a book for instance, which escapes its author and might even turn against it— no one will dispute. But we are not speaking of true creation in that case. Creation *ex nihilo,* as seen by metaphysicians and theologians, is

> the gift of existence. Consequently, a creature which would close up upon itself and make itself independent of God (assuming this were possible), would immediately cease to exist. This is what is expressed in a rather unsatisfactory manner when we say that the creature has from itself and is in itself only nothingness: all the being it has comes from God. It is absurd to imagine that a creature can become the foundation of its being after having been created. It is being created at every moment of its existence, which means that it is permanently dependent on God. A being which is the foundation of its being, which carries its causality within itself, such a being is God. And God does not become *a se,* he is.[24]

But if the creature is "permanently dependent on God," this does not mean that it is resorbed by divine thought. The concept of creation does not imply that the Creator communicate his own existence, as pantheism would have it. In Sartre's hypothesis

> the creature would not be distinct from God, if it did not recover itself. But there is another concept which cuts this alternative short and which is the right one in our opinion: existence as an act proportional to essence —the existence of God cannot be communicated, but God makes creatures exist each one in its own way and

according to its possibilities. Each one therefore has its own existence and exercises the act of being, of which God is the source.[25]

This does not mean that the world is no longer contingent. We must even say that not only does creation respect contingency, but it also founds and explains it. For the world does not emanate from the divine substance and cannot be deduced from it as a consequence from its cause. "The act of creation is free. If we start with the world, rigorous analysis reveals God as its cause—but if we start with God, we do not find the world."[26]

Here again, we are far from Sartre. But we must acknowledge that he does not dwell upon the subject of creation. And why should he, since it is a purely gratuitous hypothesis? Since God, in his view, does not and cannot exist?

We are well acquainted with the main lines of a now famous argumentation. God does not exist because, if he did, it is man who would not exist, with his freedom and his anguish. God cannot exist, because the concept of the In-itself-For-itself by which he would be defined is contradictory. Moreover, the reasoning which leads theologians and metaphysicians toward him has no other value than that which they bestow upon it. It is a freely chosen human enterprise, so that it is through us, through our choice, that "all foundations and all reasons come to being." There is no universe outside of the human universe and it is within this universe alone that the concept of God becomes meaningful, if it must have a meaning.[27]

These affirmations are most certainly of the greatest importance, but they are simply the exploitation and the logical consequence of the hypothesis which dominates the thought of Sartre from the very beginning. They are valid only in relation to this hypothesis. It is because Sartre first posited the absurdity of being and made it an in-itself, that the concept of God became contradictory and that man—by the same stroke—was referred back to himself, to his value-creating freedom, and to his irrational choices.

Sartre said his first and last word in this matter when he proclaimed that Being is wholly contingency and gratuity. Now we do not accept this word. It was presented as the expression of a metaphysical experience, whereas we feel it is but an arbitrary interpretation of this intuition.

The Intuition of Being and Its Implications

We therefore turn once more to the intuition of being. Jacques Maritain will help us, in a striking fashion, to understand the encounter of thought with Being.

> Once a man is awakened to the reality of existence and the true life of Reason, to the intelligible value of Being, once he has really perceived this tremendous fact, sometimes exhilarating, sometimes disgusting and maddening: *I exist*, he is henceforth taken hold of by the intuition of Being and the implications it involves.
>
> Precisely speaking, this prime intuition is both the intuition of *my* existence and of the existence *of things*; but first and foremost of the existence of things. When it takes place, I suddenly realize that a given entity, man, mountain, or tree, exists and exercises that sovereign activity *to be* in its own way, in an independence from *me* which is total, totally self-assertive and totally implacable. And at the same time, I realize that I also exist, but as thrown back into my loneliness and frailty

by such affirmation of existence in which I have positively no part, to which I am exactly as naught. So the prime intuition of Being is the intuition of the solidity and inexorability of existence; and, secondly, of the death and nothingness to which *my* existence is liable. And thirdly, in the same flash of intuition, which is but my becoming aware of the intelligible value of Being, I realize that the solid and inexorable existence perceived in anything whatsoever implies—I don't know yet in what way, perhaps in things themselves, perhaps separately from them—some absolute, irrefragable existence, completely free from nothingness and death. These three intellective leaps—to actual existence as asserting itself independently from me; from this sheer objective existence to my own threatened existence; and from my existence spoiled with nothingness to absolute existence —are achieved within that same and unique intuition, which philosophers would explain as the intuitive perception of the essentially analogical content of the first concept, the concept of Being.

Then a quick, spontaneous reasoning, as natural as this intuition (and, as a matter of fact, more or less involved in it) immediately springs forth, as the necessary fruit of such primordial apperception and as enforced by and under its light. That is a wordless process of reasoning, which cannot be expressed in articulate fashion without sacrificing its vital concentration and the rapidity with which it takes place. I see that my Being, first, is liable to death; and, second, that it depends on the totality of nature, on the universal whole whose part I am. I see that Being-with-nothingness, as my own being is, implies, in order to be, Being-without-nothingness—that absolute existence which I confusedly perceived as involved in my primordial intuition of existence. And I see that the universal whole, whose part I am, is Being-with-nothingness, from the very fact that I am part of it; so that finally, since the universal whole does not exist by itself, there is another Whole, a separate one, another Being, transcendent and self-sufficient and unknown in itself and activating all beings, which is Being-without-nothingness, that is, self-subsisting Being, Being existing through itself.

. . . the rediscovery of the value of exsitence not only means the rediscovery of God, it also means the rediscovery of Love. For when the intuition of Being and Existence takes place in me, it normally carries along with itself another intuition, the intuition of my own existence or my Self, the intuition of Subjectivity as Subjectivity. Now Subjectivity, insofar as it is Subjectivity, is not an object presented to thought, but rather the very wellspring of thought—a deep, unknown and living center which superabounds in knowledge and superabounds in love, attaining only through love its supreme level of existence, existence as giving itself. . . .

Thus it is that when a man has been really awakened to the sense of Being or Existence, and grasps intuitively the obscure, living depth of the Self and Subjectivity, he experiences, by virtue of the inner dynamism of this intuition, that love is not a passing pleasure or a more or less intense emotion, but the root tendency and very meaning of his being alive. He becomes both an 'ontological' and an 'erotic' man; he is man anew.

And not only does he know, by virtue of his primordial intellectual grasping of existence, that God exists and is the absolute Being, the self-subsisting *Esse*. He also knows that because of this very fact, God is absolute ontological generosity, the self-subsisting Love; and that such transcendent Love inherently causes, permeates and activates every creature, which in answer loves God more than itself. The basic love for God, this natural and universal eros, is the very virtue and innermost vitality in which all beings desire and love, act and strive.[28]

These pages, which we wish we had written, will be our conclusion. They express our fundamental disagreement with the metaphysical possibilities of a doctrine which we tried to describe with the greatest objectivity.

But it remains that we must not underestimate the testimony of Sartre, with its impassioned plea for man and his freedom. Today as yesterday, it is good that a philosopher of such stature should shake us out of our complacency and urge us to lucidity, the refusal of bad faith and the awareness of our responsibility.

NOTES

1. Colette Audry, *Connaissance de Sartre* (Paris, 1955), p. 110.
2. Francis Jeanson, *La Phénoménologie,* 2nd ed. (Paris, 1952), p. 75.
3. Henry Duméry, *Regards sur la Philosophie Contemporaine* (Paris: Tournai, 1956), pp. 181 *et seq.*
4. Jean-Paul Sartre, *Descartes* (Paris, 1946), pp. 15–16.
5. *Ibid.,* p. 28.
6. *Ibid.,* pp. 31–32.
7. *Ibid.,* pp. 32 *et seq.*
8. Jacques Maritain, *Existence and the Existent* (New York: Doubleday, 1956), p. 14.
9. Jacques Maritain, *De Bergson a Thomas d'Aquin* (Paris, 1947), p. 155.
10. *Ibid.,* p. 158.
11. *Ibid.,* pp. 162–163.
12. Jean-Marie Aubert, "La Moral Chrétienne est-elle à la Mesure de l'Homme?" *Etudes,* November 1966, pp. 515–516.
13. Jean-Paul Sartre, *Existential Psychoanalysis,* translation of several chapters of *L'Etre et le Nèant* (New York: Philosophical Library, 1953), pp. 168–188.
14. P. Ricoeur, "Aspects de la Dialectique," *Recherches de Philosophie* II, p. 129.
15. Jacques Maritain, *Existence and the Existent,* p. 29.
16. H. Payssac, *Le Dieu de Sartre,* p. 38.
17. Cf. Gilbert Varet, "L'Ontologie de Sartre"; Dominique Dubarle, "L'Ontologie Phenoménologique de Sartre," *Revue de Philosophie,* 2nd ed. (1946), pp. 90–123.
18. Jean-Paul Sartre, *Nausea* (New York: New Directions, 1964), pp. 180–181.
19. Jean-Paul Sartre, *Being and Nothingness* (New York: Citadel Press, 1966), pp. 357–543.

20. Sartre, *Nausea*, p. 176.
21. Cf. Claude Trémontant, *Comment se pose aujord'hui le problème de l'existence de Dieu?*, pp. 141–156.
22. J.-M. Cottier, *La Table Ronde*, no. 182, May 1963, p. 20.
23. Cf. Chapter I.
24. Roger Verneaux, *Leçons sur l'Athéisme Contemporain*, pp. 83–84.
25. *Ibid.*, p. 84.
26. *Ibid.*, p. 84.
27. Cf. H. Payssac, *Le Dieu de Sartre*; Régis Jolivet, *Sartre ou la Théologies de l'Absurde*; Francis Jeanson, *Les Ecrivains devant Dieu*.
28. Jacques Maritain, *The Range of Reason* (New York: Scribner's, 1952), pp. 88–92.

Index